How to Speak Furniture with an Antique English Accent

Buying, Selling and Appraisal Tips Plus Price Guides

Jeanne Siegel

Bonus Books, Inc., Chicago

This book is dedicated to its readers
who appreciate the uniqueness of English furniture

and to my English grandparents
Mary and Lewis

©**1992 by Bonus Books, Inc.**
All rights reserved

Except for appropriate use in critical reviews or works of scholarship, the reproduction or use of this work in any form or by any electronic, mechanical or other means now known or hereafter invented, including photocopying and recording, and in any information storage and retrieval system is forbidden without the written permission of the publisher.

96 95 94 93 92   5 4 3 2 1

Library of Congress Catalog Card Number: 91-77013

International Standard Book Number: 0-929387-43-0

Bonus Book, Inc.
160 East Illinois Street
Chicago, Illinois 60611

All insert illustrations by Jeanne Siegel

Printed in the United States of America

CONTENTS

ACKNOWLEDGMENTS	v
WHY THIS BOOK	1
CHRONOLOGY OF ENGLISH FURNITURE	4
INTRODUCTION TO ANTIQUE ENGLISH FURNITURE	9
ENGLISH MORSELS	12
DISTINGUISHING ENGLISH FROM AMERICAN FURNITURE	18
CLUES, CHICANERY AND CHARACTERISTICS	25
TIMBER LINES	33
WOODS	37
AUCTION TERMS	41
CLARIFICATIONS	44
TUDOR AND EARLY STUART 1485–1600	46
LATE STUART 1600–1700	50
QUEEN ANNE AND EARLY GEORGIAN 1702–1740	53
MID-GEORGIAN OR ROCOCO 1740–1765	55
LATE GEORGIAN 1765–1800	59
REGENCY 1800–1830	64
VICTORIAN 1830–1900	66
COLLECTING AND BUYING	71
PRICE GUIDE	74
SELLING	84
VOCABULARY	87
BIBLIOGRAPHY	167
INDEX	173

ACKNOWLEDGMENTS

Norman Adams, 8–10 Hans Road (opposite the West side of Harrods), London, England, for providing the photograph for the front cover.

Caledonia, Inc., 562 Lincoln Avenue, Winnetka, Illinois, for photographs. Their cooperation was very special.

Dunning's Auction House, 755 Church Road, Elgin, Illinois.

William Doyle Galleries, 175 East 87th Street, New York, New York. Thank you Diane M. Waters.

Leslie Hindman Auctioneers, 215 West Ohio Street, Chicago, Illinois.

The Victoria and Albert Museum, in London, where I spent many happy hours, and the beautiful Georgian city of Bath.

An overdue thank you for my friend, Alan Choka, who encouraged me from the beginning.

My appreciation to Claudette Giss who has done another great secretarial job.

WHY THIS BOOK

I am an American writing about English furniture. This book closes the circle I began with my first book on American furniture. Because American furniture, and its history, has many similarities to English furniture, I was led to focus my second book on furniture developed in one specific period of English history—the Victorian period. Now I have come full circle and am writing on English furniture—its history and its characteristics.

Americans have a strong English heritage. American history and antique American furniture have a close relationship with their English counterparts. But many differences do exist. I take advantage of knowledge from my previous books as well as new research to point out similar and divergent characteristics in the two countries' furniture. Knowing these differences and similarities can save, and make, you money. For example, an English Queen Anne side chair with a round pad foot might be sold to a collector as a Massachusetts chair because it also has a round pad foot. But these two chairs are not equal in value. Knowing that English oak usually darkens while American oak retains its golden color will aid in identifying and pricing furniture.

Need more examples? English painted chairs parallel to American "fancy" chairs often had upholstered seats while American chairs did not. English japanned pieces were often displayed on ornately carved and gilded stands with matching tops while American japanned pieces were not presented in this way.

Antique English furniture vocabulary is not the same as antique American or antique French vocabulary. The same word will often have different meanings. English "bureaus" and "davenports" usually refer to desks and "looking glass" to "mirrors." The definition of an English slipper foot can differ from that of an American one. And the term "shoulder piece," used to describe part of an English chair, is not used when describing American furniture. Differences even exist in the vocabulary used to describe the furniture in different periods within the same country's history. Therefore, it is necessary to know and understand the differences in the vocabulary used when describing various types of antique furniture.

English furniture was influenced by the desires of her rulers in Medieval times, by the Church and by existing social conditions. English pieces made for the crown are called "court furniture." Americans, having no courts or palaces, had no court furniture. There are no American "Brighton Pavilions."

The English refer to their furniture periods by using the names of significant ruling monarchs. None of the eight American furniture periods are named for presidents, but three periods are named for English designers—Chippendale, Hepplewhite, and Sheraton—and one period for Queen Victoria.

English period names can be confusing. For example, the Regency furniture period is 1800 to 1830, but George IV was actually acting as regent from 1811 to 1820. The Victorian furniture period begins in 1830 withstanding the fact that Victoria was not queen until 1837. This is why I have included a chart of English periods, monarchs and characteristics.

The English made their greatest furniture ornate. Americans made their greatest furniture simple. Americans, however, have always admired and collected beautifully crafted English pieces made for the middle and upper classes. George Washington's Mount Vernon is a prime example of English furniture in an American home.

The cost of fine new furniture is such that antique English furniture is a sound investment as well as pleasurable and historic (see price guide). Happily English craftsmen created an abundance of excellent furniture and many prime examples are still available for contemporary use. One of the reasons for this abundance was the well furnished English country house. Such houses represented more than pride of ownership. Land was the basis of prestige and political power, and many of these estates occupied several hundred thousands of acres. Until 1906 country house owners formed a majority in every British cabinet.

Antique furniture did not begin with the English. Various early civilizations had superb furniture. It is evident from carvings, paintings and tombs, that Egypt, China and Greece enjoyed exquisite beds, chairs, chests and stools. Many techniques, such as dovetailing, were perfected by the ancient Egyptians. Elegant Tang dynasty pieces had, what we call, cabriole legs. Greek vase paintings illustrate tables, couches and the timeless klismos chair. These periods are worth studying in themselves.

However, this book deals only with English furniture which originated in the Middle Ages and reached maturity in the eighteenth century. The emphasis will be on Georgian furniture. Included are the major English furniture periods starting with the Tudor and ending with the close of the Victorian age.

I attempt to give some historical background notes which are morsels of early English life. I describe many differences between English and American furniture, give clues, characteristics, chicanery facts and clarifications. This is also a book about words. The vocabulary is not only for looking up words; it is a "labor of love." If you start with the A's and keep reading, you will have the sound and vision of antique English furniture.

The purpose of this book is similar to that of my previous books. My desire is to provide a comprehensive English furniture language for description, identification, and as a valuable tool in the art of buying, selling and collecting.

The buyer should have the vocabulary to ask pertinent questions, command respect and use auction catalogues and price guides to their best advantage. The seller must be able to give customers accurate and beautiful descriptions. Collectors require the ability to describe their collections with loving accuracy. Therefore, the right word is all important!

Descriptive words enrich our furniture experience, hence, this book aids in reading other books by taking the mystery out of the words many authors use, but don't explain.

The study of English furniture is a showcase for their craftsmen, whether early arkwright or master eighteenth century cabinetmaker. I hope this book will provide the words that will allow you to speak this furniture with an antique English accent.

CHRONOLOGY OF ENGLISH FURNITURE

(All periods have transitional elements
and may overlap the reigns of several rulers)

Early Tudor — 1485-1558

Rulers — Henry VII.............1485-1509
Henry VIII............1509-1547
Edward VI............1547-1553
Mary I................1553-1558

Features — Plain, sturdy, boxy forms, usually rectangular. Gothic style of carving. Also, Renaissance motifs, linen-fold panelling, strapwork and paint.

Woods — Oak, elm.

Late Tudor/Early Stuart — 1560-1600

Rulers — Elizabeth I............1559-1603
James I...............1603-1625

Features — Jacobean designs, sturdy, carved, ornaments, bulbous supports, geometric panels, arcading, Oriental motifs and paint.

Woods — Oak, walnut, elm (for inlay of bog oak), holly, poplar.

Chronology of English Furniture

Late Stuart — 1600-1700

Rulers — Charles I 1626-1649
　　　　　　　　　　　　　Carolean is a term applicable to pieces made in the reign of Charles I
　　　　　　Charles II . . . . .Crowned 1649 and again in 1661 after Restoration
　　　　　　James II 1685-1688
　　　　　　William III 1689-1702
　　　　　　Mary II 1689-1694

Features — Dramatic highs and lows, thicks and thins, scrolls, carved ornaments, Braganza feet, bun feet, spiral turnings, ornate or curved stretchers, cup turnings, inlay, parquetry, marquetry, lacquer and gilding.

Woods — Walnut (solid or as veneer), beech or maple. For veneering, yew, elm and mulberry. For oyster veneer laburnum, olive or walnut. Limewood for carving.

Commonwealth and Protectorate — 1649-1659

Rulers — Lord Protector — Oliver Cromwell
　　　　　　Lord Protector — Richard Cromwell

Features — Puritan values; utilitarian. Simple decorative furniture, leather, brass-headed nails.

Woods — Oak.

How to Speak Furniture with an Antique English Accent

Queen Anne/Early Georgian — 1702-1740

Rulers — Anne 1702-1714
George I 1714-1727
George II 1727-1760

Features — Simple lines, curvilinear form, cabriole leg, Dutch feet, paw feet, shell motif, hoop-back, gilding, Oriental influences, lacquering and limited carving. Later features – open splats decorated with narrow vertical cuts, lion and satyr heads, honeysuckle, winged satyrs, cabochons, leaf designs, paw feet, ball-and-claw feet.

Woods — Walnut, solid or veneer. Mahogany introduced in 1725.

Mid-Georgian or Rococo — 1740-1765

Rulers — George II 1727-1760
George III 1761-1820

Features — Many influences: French, Chinese, Rococo. Return to Gothic designs, Chippendale designs, fine carving, ball-and-claw feet and lattice-work. Adam Neo-Classical designs emerging.

Woods — Mahogany (solid or veneer), satinwood and yew wood. Use of walnut declining.

Chronology of English Furniture

Late Georgian — 1765-1800

Rulers — George III...............1761-1820

Features — Neo-Classical designs, tapering legs, Adam, Sheraton, Hepplewhite, painted decoration.

Woods — Mahogany, satinwood (solid and veneer), inlay, rosewood, sycamore and white holly.

Regency — 1800-1830

Rulers — George IV ....Regent 1811-1820
King 1821-1830
William IV 1831-1837

Features — Decorative veneers, ebonizing, gold enrichments, brass inlay, cast metal feet, lion-mask mounts, Chinese designs, cane.

Woods — Rosewood, mahogany, painted beech.

Victorian — 1830-1900

Ruler — Victoria 1837-1901

Features — Many revival designs, Regency, Louis XIV, Louis XV, Elizabethan, Gothic, Oriental, rattan, cane, bentwood, Arts and Crafts designs, cast-iron.

Woods — Rosewood, mahogany, amboyna, satinwood, oak, walnut.

INTRODUCTION TO ANTIQUE ENGLISH FURNITURE

English furniture is no stranger. We have seen it through the eyes of Henry James, Charles Dickens, Robin Hood and the Sheriff of Nottingham, Sherlock Holmes, William Shakespeare and Scarlett O'Hara, who like other rich Southerners, imported their furniture from England.

English furniture has a presence that reminds us of the character and appearance of the people who used it. Homes of men and women, then as now, are not merely places to live in, but a statement of self and social worth.

Furniture, whether antique or contemporary, is rooted in existing universal designs that emerged in antiquity. We see how man is drawn, over and over, to particular uses, shapes and details.

From early tribal cultures to the present, material objects incorporating universal designs have satisfied some of our human needs. While the English cabinetmaker was using the herringbone design for banding veneered pieces, Bedouin tribes were using the herringbone design on their weavings. Basic designs are found throughout the world and in all eras to decorate, whether on camel bags or furniture.

Northern Europe did not develop a civilized society like Egypt, China and Greece. Life in Britain, a rather foggy isolated island, was rough and primitive. Not until Medieval times did the situation slowly improve. Native culture was influenced by the wars and occupation of foreigners, including Scots, Normans and Romans. Even the fortunate had little more than their clothes, perhaps a ring or necklace, and a storage chest. These meager possessions, however, were embellished with embroidery, polishing or simple carving, indicating a desire for beauty.

As greater political stability was achieved, castles and towns took root and craftsmen began to make furniture to satisfy the needs and wishes of the rich and powerful.

The earliest known painted portrait of an English sovereign

is that of Richard II (1377-1399), painted about 1398. Richard, depicted with crown and scepter, dressed in ermine and fine robes, is seated on a Gothic style throne. The crest-rail is carved with trefoils and the back stiles rise high with pinnacle finials. The chair as well as the man indicate importance.

Almost a century would elapse, however, before fine English furniture would be made for other than the crown, the church and the well placed.

This book begins with the early Tudor period of King Henry VII. Columbus will not sail for America for thirty-three years. The furniture of this period had boxy forms, Gothic designs and Renaissance motifs, but much more was to come.

We will follow styles and designs that flower in the eighteenth century, continue to develop into the Victorian period, and then revert to boxy forms, Gothic designs and Renaissance motifs of the Arts and Crafts Movement.

English furniture bloomed in the eighteenth century. William and Mary taste influenced by Dutch, Portuguese and French designs brought drama to replace previous boxy styles. These pieces with their dramatic carvings, caning, twists, japanning and veneering infused English design with variety and glamour. Queen Anne furniture brought grace and comfort with curves that followed the human shape, elegant cabriole legs with pad, paw and subsequently ball-and-claw feet, domed cabinets with looking glass and upholstered furniture. The Georgian years are valued for the designs and work of Adam, Chippendale, Hepplewhite and Sheraton, who created masterpieces from mahogany, satinwood and rosewood. Georgian furniture continues to delight collectors who chose to furnish their homes with antique English furniture.

English furniture has survived fires, wars and carelessness, but what remains are solid, beautifully crafted pieces. Like all world furniture, English pieces echo the ancient world and outside influences including invasions, trade and the crusades. Thus, while Dutch, Italian, Portuguese, as well as ancient Greek and Chinese influences appear, the result is peculiarly and beautifully English. Just looking at this furniture you know it is not Italian, French, Scandinavian, German or Russian. Only the Americans copied it faithfully, however, they brought their own national character to these existing designs.

Antique English furniture is timeless. It is the past, the present and the future.

ENGLISH MORSELS

A carpenter's guild has existed in England since the early fourteenth century.

Modesty was not a medieval characteristic, and privacy was almost unknown. These folks shared their beds, usually pallets, with one another—brothers, sisters, servants, guests, and even strangers—and most did it naked. Later, retiring rooms were provided for women, imitating Oriental harems the crusaders had observed.

A large or important house was called "The Hall." Often at one end of its central room (the great hall) a platform was erected for the master and perhaps his guests. On this platform (dais) would be a chair for the master of the house, or if his guest was of higher rank, the guest was accorded the chair and his host sat on a stool. A table might also be on this platform, and eventually a serving piece. Less important guests or family members would have stools or benches, and a trestle table might be set up for their use below the platform.

Chairs were reserved for important men. This is the origin of the expression "chairman" signifying the man in the chair, who sat at the board (table). We still refer to a "chairman of the board" as an important person in business or colloquially.

The tripod stool was common in the late Middle Ages, but chairs as domestic pieces were not in common use until the seventeenth century.

The lady of the house would be accommodated with a stool.

During Medieval times the most common trencher (plate), even for the wealthy, was a slab of stale bread. Since the bread was porous, two or more cloths were used to catch the drippings. The cloth closest to the table would be the best one.

The chest or "chist" was the basic furniture piece of the Medieval period. These pieces were used in the home or carried about when the household travelled. Domed lids were designed to curtail rain and snow leaks—imitating water off a duck's back.

The chest is perhaps the only fourteenth century or even earlier piece that has survived.

The elaborate carving found on exceptional fourteenth century chests was accomplished by independent wood sculptors, not the carpenters or arkwrights, who also carved Church screens.

After 1500, rich textiles indicated wealth and power. There were bed hangings, table carpets, cupboard cloths (cup-board cloths), wall hangings and floor coverings (carpets). Early carpets were stored and only laid on important occasions.

Chairs with wrought-iron frames were made by blacksmiths in the fifteenth century.

The expression "a square peg in a round hole" comes from early English furniture construction. Square, tapering pegs of green wood were pounded into round holes as a simple method of joining. It worked contrary to how we interpret the expression today.

Upholstered pieces do not appear until Elizabethan times.

From the mid-1500s, Gothic pieces were inlaid with holly, bog oak, and various stained woods. This inlay had Flemish or German roots.

Furniture of the Gothic period was made by craftsmen such as arkwrights.

The floors in medieval halls were often laid with white clay and covered with layers of rushes. Sweet smelling herbs were dropped on them to mask vile odors.

The kitchen cupboard (dresser) was a new piece in the late Stuart period. It was designed in two parts. The top, with a high back, had long narrow shelves, and the lower portion had enclosed cupboards with a row of drawers above and a long wide surface for carving. They were often of solid oak and held an amazing amount of dishes and pewter.

From Medieval times until the mid-seventeenth century, fire screens were often of wicker basketwork and usually circular.

The English dressing table emerged about 1660 in wealthy homes. We tend to regard the dressing table as a woman's piece of furniture, but a fashionable Englishman was as vain as his wife or mistress.

The earliest corner cupboards date from pre-Restoration days (Charles I).

In the Stuart period, rooms were set aside as "parlours," and furnished with appropriate pieces.

Furniture for the royal family was called "court furniture." It was much richer in design and materials than pieces made for the wealthy. America is the only country that had no court furniture. They had no court.

When William and Mary ruled England, the queen indulged her passion for collecting Oriental porcelain. This passion led to the development of glazed cabinets to display objects.

Coffee arrived as a drink in 1645; chocolate in 1657; and tea in 1658; countless tables were designed on which to serve these new beverages.

Queen Anne was known for her love of elegantly curved furniture. She must also have loved children, as she bore nineteen. Loving subjects called her "good Queen Anne."

Various Queen Anne chairs had ivory inlay.

The Windsor chair made its appearance in the Queen Anne period.

The fashion for chinoiserie (shēn wäz ə rē) was prevalent from the early seventeenth century to the early twentieth century. This style, identified as Chinese, was characterized by intricate patterns and an extensive use of motifs. The chinoiserie furniture design reoccurred at periods of about fifty years. The fashion for it dates from about 1610 to 1620. The second period dates from after the restoration of the monarchy in 1660. The third was in the mid-eighteenth century when designers such as Thomas Chippendale used Chinese motifs with complete surrender. The fourth era was when the Prince of Wales, later prince regent in the early years of the nineteenth century, personally championed the style and expressed his appreciation for it in his pavilion at Brighton. The fifth interval occurred in the Victorian period.

Early in the seventeenth century a piece of furniture, having much in common with the court cupboard, was developed in Wales. It is called a Welsh dresser. This Welsh dresser had a pronounced cornice finished with corner pendants projecting above the shelving (an obvious link with the court cupboard), and a cupboard or pot rack in the lower portion.

In the seventeenth century, a "flower pott" could be a vase, but it could also be a large urn with handles.

In the dining room, a chamber pot was kept handy in a cupboard of the sideboard until the early Victorian period when water closets came into use.

Artificial flowers made of paper, feathers and silk, were a form of decoration during the seventeenth century.

Barbados, the easternmost and most English of the Caribbean Islands, was settled by the British in 1625, and remained a British possession until 1958. From 1658, furniture based on English designs—most of local cedar wood—was produced there. During the eighteenth century, a large quantity of furniture was also imported from London. The English designs used or imported were generally the more simple, country style variety. Antiquarians have carried off these pieces whenever they located them.

The Great Fire of London in 1666 burned 13,200 houses to the ground in four days. Lumber yards within the city were also destroyed and timber from the American colonies became a necessity.

The Shakers left England in 1774 to escape religious persecution, but their finely designed American furniture has inescapable English roots.

The Tatler, in 1710, suggested that the sumptuous sideboard has more often "the Air of an Altar" than a table. It was the custom in the eighteenth century to remove the table cloth for the dessert course. In the nineteenth century, it was considered too much trouble.

The Cromwellian chair epitomized the barrenness of the puritanical Commonwealth Period. The chair, four squared and rigid, offered little comfort or beauty. It had a straight back, the members were rarely sausage-turned, and the back and seat were often bare of upholstery. About the time of the Restoration, the chair's unimaginative turnings were given a crisp, spiral "Portuguese twist" and the back and seat soon began to be made of cane.

The dining room played an important role in English Georgian lifestyle. It is said they were called "apartments of conversation." This room was a male preserve where the gentlemen remained for hours after the women had withdrawn to the drawing room. The drawing room was the ladies' province.

An English barber's chair (circa 1780) was similar to a

roundabout or corner chair but can be identified by an additional splat, within uprights or solid shape superposed on the top-rail of the back. It looks like a small chair back above a normal one. An interesting piece.

The "Beau Brummel" is a late eighteenth century piece named for the dandy of the same name. It was a dressing table in demi-lune (half circle) shape usually made of satinwood. Its mirror and its supports rise from a shallow shaped compartment at the back. Its tapered legs are castored.

Thomas Chippendale was the son of a joiner and spent his youth making plain country furniture. He was the first English craftsman to publish a furniture pattern book, *The Gentleman and Cabinet-Makers Directory*. One of his famous clients was the Shakespearean actor and director, David Garrick, who dominated the London stage. Mr. Garrick lived "like a prince" in his villa at Hampton. As I recall, Shakespeare's princes did not have things so good.

Thomas Chippendale, like all great artists, worried about his creations. In a letter dated December 27, 1766, he begged Sir Rowland Winn not to transport his masterpiece writing table and his magnificent clothes press by water. His patron eventually agreed and conveyed them by wagon. They arrived safely.

It is interesting that cabinetmakers such as Chippendale regularly provided customers, free of charge, with watercolor renderings showing the design and disposition for furniture, whereas architects, such as Adam, charged a fee for them.

Eighteenth century ladies enjoyed using pattern books as coloring books.

English rent tables are a late eighteenth century innovation. They evolved from the counting board or counting chest used by shops. These tables were originally plain tables made in a circular, hexagonal or octagonal "drum" shape. They had a revolving top fitted with drawers in the frieze, and were generally mounted on a pillar and four footed base. In the Regency period, the circular hexagonal or octagonal table on pillar-and-claws, or a central pedestal was described as a library table.

Thomas Sheraton was a poor man who died in poverty. How poor was he? Adams Black, the future publisher of *Encyclopaedia Britannica* visited him in London, and relates that "he [Sheraton] lived in an obscure street. His house half shop, [he] looked like a worn-out Methodist minister, with a threadbare black coat. I took tea with them. There were a cup and saucer for the host, another for his wife, and a little porringer for their daughter. The wife's cup and saucer were given to me and she had to put up with a little porringer." How very sad.

Under the dining room table, a "drugget" was placed. This was a wool or linen cloth used to catch crumbs. Even Queen Victoria used a drugget at Balmoral.

The Victorian sideboard was also called the "drink board" because this is where the decanters and wine bottles were placed.

The origin of an object could determine style. During the reign of Charles II, when tea drinking became fashionable, tea services and japanned tea tables were decorated in Chinese style. In the Victorian period, the "smoking room" where men could indulge their taste for cigars and pipes were often designed in Turkish style because the best tobacco came from Turkey.

George I was unpopular perhaps due to the fact he had two German mistresses. He made one a countess and the other a duchess. Another problem was his inability to speak English.

George II was the last British sovereign to lead troops into battle (Battle of Dettingen in the War of the Austrian succession).

George III was associated with tyranny at home and in America. He had intermittent periods of insanity starting from 1780, and in 1810 became permanently insane.

George IV, while the Prince of Wales and regent, was the leader of a profligate society. As king he was hated for his extravagance and dissolute habits.

William IV was called "Silly Billy."

Victoria's consort, Prince Albert, was the president of the Society of Arts. Perhaps this interest passed to his remote grandson, the present Prince of Wales who has become identified with questions of architecture and design in modern Britain.

Edward VII, Victoria's eldest son, had his own specially made furniture for lovemaking. Pieces like a siege d'amour (love chair) were made in the Rococo style. This piece was designed to amuse him with two ladies at the same time. It is known as bordello furniture.

DISTINGUISHING ENGLISH FROM AMERICAN FURNITURE

English and American furniture have great similarities, and the closeness of many pieces can be astonishing.

English Jacobean pieces might have had pearl inlays, but American Puritan pieces did not.

Heavily carved wainscot chairs are English.

English Jacobean cupboards often used carved griffins or mythical creatures as supports, while American Puritan cupboards used only bulbous turnings. (American griffins came in the Empire period.)

William and Mary cane topped tables and cane chairs, with animal feet, are English.

Square, cabriole legs are not American, but are found on English William and Mary pieces.

William and Mary cane chairs with faces on their knees are English.

During the second half of the seventeenth century, the English used narrow boards on their chair-tables since lumber was becoming scarce. Their American counterparts used wide boards as they had full forests.

Another English trait in the William and Mary period is double-domed tops on tall casepieces like secretaries.

English Queen Anne secretaries had their doors inset with looking glass, while American Queen Anne secretaries usually had solid wood doors. However, as all furniture was commissioned, there are rare examples of looking glass in American doors. This trait was passed on to the Chippendale style secretaries in which the English continued to have looking glass doors; the American, wood.

English Queen Anne chairs sometimes terminate the rear legs in squared hoof feet. This is not an American trait.

Various English Queen Anne chairs have modified block Spanish feet (Braganza) on the rear legs, whereas the Americans used the Spanish foot only on the front legs.

English Queen Anne pad feet are more circular than American ones.

English slipper feet are usually more rounded than American slipper feet which tend to be more pointed.

The English often refer to a Dutch snake foot as a slipper foot, and what Americans simply call a slipper foot as a pointed slipper, a pointed pad or a pointed foot. This can be confusing, especially in catalogues.

Large American pieces such as secretaries or highboys are seldom as large as English ones.

English casepieces are usually taller and wider than American ones.

American furniture parts, called members, are usually heavier and sturdier than English parts.

Tight, sausage turnings seen on stretchers are usually found on furniture from America or the Netherlands.

The English seventeenth century chest on a stand with drawers, a shaped apron, turned legs, and flat stretchers was copied with such fidelity in the New England states of America that only by identifying the wood can the origin be verified.

Both the English and Americans (circa 1730) often straightened out the cabriole leg into a straight-turned leg with a round pad foot. Examples are found on tables.

The use of a single straight rear stretcher on eighteenth century chairs with cabriole legs is an English trait.

English backboards were vertically placed, varied in width and often butt-joined. American backboards were often simply nailed in place.

Exposed backboards darken with age but enclosed drawers do not.

English drawers were constructed with thin boards of oak or deal. Deal was thin boards of scotch fir (also called wild pine). English drawers almost without exception had thin oak bottoms. American drawers were constructed with thick boards of poplar (which have a distinctive greenish stripe), pine and chestnut. American Queen Anne and Chippendale drawer bottoms were often of white cedar that resembles pine with small knots. English pieces repaired in America will have the thick American woods. If you are identifying a piece with drawers, check each one.

English carving is usually more rounded in profile than American carving. English chairs are more likely to have carving, such as an English Chippendale chair with Gothic style carving.

Carving on English Chippendale claw-and-ball feet are usually more richly detailed than on American ones.

Marquetry with ivory, dyed woods or bone is likely to be Continental rather than English or American.

Many fine antique English pieces were made of American Virginia walnut. It was exported to England beginning in 1720 after the Great Fire of London.

Early English and American Windsors were painted (often green), not stained.

English Windsors often had pierced ornamental back splats. American ones usually had backs composed entirely of spindles, but occasionally some are seen with arches.

English Windsors often had cabriole legs with pad feet. American Windsors did not except in very rare instances.

Late English Victorian Windsors became much larger, heavier, top-heavy, and more complex, than American Victorian Windsors.

English japanned pieces were heavily decorated while American pieces were executed with a lighter hand.

English pieces have their chinoiserie designs built up with gesso. Americans did not use gesso, but occasionally used whiting (crushed chalk).

English japanned pieces were often displayed on ornately

carved and gilded stands and might have carved matching tops. This was not an American trait.

English Chippendale tripod pie-crust tables have the entire "pie" carved to resemble a Chinese dish.

Cabochons with foliage are found, at the knee, on English 1740s cabriole legs. Americans didn't favor cabochons on their knees, but some, usually smaller, appear on certain Philadelphia Chippendale chairs and on a variety of English and American Victorian pieces.

Ribbon-back Chippendale style chairs are English. These very fancy chairs were not made in America. A simpler ribbon design was made in Maryland, Pennsylvania and New York.

American cabriole legs are often "over curved" by English standards.

Claw-and-ball feet with eagle's claws are more apt to be American. The English preferred dragon claws.

The English mirror had the backboard cut inside the framing, while the American custom was to make the backboard larger than the opening and nail it to the frame.

Molding back posts and the crest-rail to two distinct lines is an English practice. This occurs when the vertical lines of a chair's back stile extend to form the ears while the crest-rail form begins inside the stile. The opposite occurs when the crest-rail form extends to include the ears and the back stiles are a distinct separate form. Examples are found in the eighteenth century.

English Hepplewhite commodes had painted decorations, elaborate marquetry and gilt brass (ormolu) mounts. American Hepplewhite pieces were much plainer.

Both England and America had Hepplewhite spade feet, but chairs with carved spade feet are English.

English shield-back chairs can have a block foot as well as a spade foot. American shield-back chairs usually have a straight leg or a spade foot.

Certain Hepplewhite chairs, both English and American, have inlaid cuffs on their legs.

English Hepplewhite shield-back chairs usually have a lower center on their shields than their American counterparts.

English Georgian Hepplewhite painted chairs were decorated with painted ribbons and flowers. Painted chairs, called "fancy chairs," became important in America during the Sheraton period (which followed their Hepplewhite period). English painted chairs often had upholstered seats while American chairs did not.

Hepplewhite introduced the tambour feature on some desks and secretary bookcases. The term "tambour" refers to a series of small strips of wood glued on a piece of canvas or strong cloth in a manner as to produce a flexible sheet. Both English and American pieces were made with the tambour feature.

The English and the Americans designed tall casepieces with removable legs. They may have travelled more safely but could be a problem to assemble and often required some refinishing.

The English, from 1730 to 1740, made Palladian style tables with gray marble tops, carved with Roman motifs, masks, shells and garlands. Americans did not make this type of table.

Americans did not make furniture decked with Rococo fantasy until the late nineteenth century, and then it was less fantastic.

Americans did not carve monsters on their furniture until the late Victorian period, and then not as heavily or often as the English.

The carving on English chairs with retracted claws is more richly detailed than on most American chairs.

Furniture designed with block fronts is characteristic of the Americans, French, Germans, Scandinavians and Italians—not the English.

English casepieces with long drawers usually have wood partitions between the drawers (dust-boards). These boards kept a thief from putting a hand through an unlocked drawer into a locked one. Most American pieces do not have this detail, although Virginia was the exception and a Boston cabinetmaker is known to have used them.

Antique English chairs incorporate the chair splat into the shoe which fits into the rear seat-rail. Chairs without a shoe are often judged modern, but this is not always the case. While Americans followed this design, other countries like Ireland constructed chairs, in English taste, without a shoe.

Both the English Gainsborough chair and the American Martha Washington chair are alike. They are both high back upholstered chairs with open arms. The Gainsborough chair was named for the English painter who sat many of his subjects in them and the Martha Washington chair was named for America's first lady.

The two basic forms of corner blocks (seat bracing) found on English chairs also appear on American chairs.

In England, it is usual to have the piece of wood forming the seat-rail drop down behind the brackets. This trait is also found on various Philadelphia chairs.

On English Sheraton sideboards the handle bases are usually round. On American Sheraton sideboards the handle bases are usually oval.

Many English Sheraton pieces combined gilt, inlay, and complete paintings, often by famous artists of the period like Angelia Kauffman, Cipriana and Pergolese. American Sheraton pieces never reached this degree of decoration.

English and American tall chests, during the English Georgian and American Chippendale and Federal periods, frequently had friezes and cornices at the top, often employing fret-work. However, the English pieces were often more elaborate.

The English made entire pieces from satinwood, but Americans did not.

The rocking chair, invented by Ben Franklin, is uniquely American! Subsequently, the English used them for women and invalids. It wasn't until Thonet designed his bentwood rocker that these chairs became popular in England.

English mounts, made for English use, were generally larger than those made for the American market. The exception would be mounts for block front pieces that were made in Newport, Rhode Island. English mounts were more highly decorated and ornate than American mounts, as their furniture was also often more ornate.

The English, in particular, made decorative nursery screens from cutouts which were then shellacked. English Victorian screens are now sought after for contemporary rooms. If in good condition, these pieces, originally made by nannies, now demand high prices at prestigious showrooms. The "nursery" was not an American tradition.

Both English and American Victorian furniture leaned on existing periods and styles such as Tudor, Stuart and Elizabethan. Gothic Revival was more important in all of England's rooms, while American Gothic Revival styles were usually confined to the hall or library.

English Victorian furniture had more elaborate ormolu and contrasting woods than American Victorian pieces.

Loo tables have the distinct possibility of being English.

Large sideboards panelled and inlaid with mottled English oak and carved in ornate Renaissance styles are English. Americans also carved large Renaissance style pieces.

Mid-Victorian secretaries entirely veneered in tulip wood with elaborate ormolu mounts and oak drawer linings are English.

Papier-mache pieces with their painted floral decorations, gold enrichments, mother-of-pearl and painted picture panels are English. The home of the papier-mache trade was Birmingham.

"Anglo-Japanese" aesthetic pieces with sloping roof tops (pagoda-like), Oriental arrangement of mirrors, panels, squared legs, fret-work and ebonizing are English.

CLUES, CHICANERY AND CHARACTERISTICS

First impressions are often the best. If you love it, it will fit in.

The collector looks for what is beautiful. The appraiser looks first for what is wrong. If we find too many "wrongs," sometimes it is no longer beautiful.

If the piece is in the thousands, a secretary or a dining table, consider an hour of an appraiser's time.

We can't always afford what we love, but if we really look at the piece and really remember it, then it is ours forever.

The more you handle antique furniture, touch, measure with your eyes, rub your fingers over, and mentally compare with similar pieces, the quicker you'll develop instinct. Instinct is important! The beauty of old walnut patinas, the soft edges of true antique pieces, the cold velvet of old marble.... If I see "harsh tones, sharp edges or yogurt" instead of "cold velvet," I back off.

We are collecting antique English furniture, so we ask.... Is the piece English? Are we sure?

What is the approximate date when made?

Is that date the period it actually belongs to? (A very important point.)

Has it been altered? "Is this fine commode really a gussied-up chest?"

Can I see any visible age, soft edges, wear, cracks or repairs? If not, I doubt its age.

If a piece has "your name on it," you'll get it. Some things are meant to be ours, some are not.

What is a proper description? Example: "An English desk circa 1830, Regency period, kidney shaped, veneered in nicely patinated yew wood, panelled with box wood and ebony inlay, ornamented with finely chased mounts and beadings, leather top not original. Price $."

Appreciate dealers with fine, very deserved reputations who have remained in business for many years. If an honest mistake is made or if you want to upgrade or sell back, these dealers will try to oblige. They are usually delighted to get one of their earlier pieces back.

Always buy from a shop's owner if possible. An assistant usually cannot negotiate the price lower than 10 per cent. Often the owner will, depending on the original cost to him, how long it has been unsold, or if a loan was required to buy it. It never hurts to bargain.

Ask for a written description, including the price, of your purchase on the shop letterhead. This is important in case the piece is stolen, damaged by a moving company or a fire. Your heirs will also appreciate this.

Most dealers keep a polaroid camera on hand; if so, ask for a picture. If not, photograph your antique furniture yourself. Keep copies in a safe deposit box.

I encourage you to frequent auction houses. Viewing is an important "hands-on" learning tool. If you are concerned with the reputation of the auction house, check with an estate lawyer or an appraiser. Auction houses are important to us whether we are the buyer or the seller.

Buying at charity sales may allow you a tax write-off, but if it is not what you really want, you will never enjoy the piece.

Be cautious at private sales (like house sales). They can be salted with phonies by the private party or by the sales agent, especially at an impressive home. However, small house sales with inexperienced agents can be a great source of joy. Arrive early and head for the basement where wonderful heavy pieces may be waiting for you. It helps if you're big. I lost a great chair when a really big guy said "I touched it first."

Decorators have a reputation of marketing quasi-antiques, but don't tar them all with the same brush. Again, whatever you buy, get a written description under a letterhead.

No one fakes an inexpensive piece, or a readily available authentic piece. For instance, antique Victorian furniture is not scarce, so it is not faked. However, the nonfaked piece of today may be the faked piece of tomorrow. There are fashions in antique furniture, and if the originals are not around, then the fake is.

Since a set of six or eight antique chairs is more expensive than a set of four, a faker will take four original chairs apart, make new parts (members) and assemble the four into six or eight chairs with intermingled parts.

Faked pieces are more often composed of antique fragments than made of new woods.

Misrepresenting the origin of a piece for profit is a form of fakery. For example, when a knowledgeable dealer sells an English side chair as a more valuable Massachusetts side chair.

A faked piece will be "tight," while an antique piece "gives." This is because wood shrinks with age so the joints will be looser.

"All original" is fantastic and probably unrealistic.

Look at furniture you are considering in good light. If possible, take the piece outside.

Carefully study the entire piece: the legs, bottom, top, sides and back, including the cornice or pediment. Request a ladder if necessary.

Remove every drawer. Check the drawer runners. The inside condition will indicate repairs, remodeling and any other changes.

Ask to have all known repairs pointed out.

If a piece has "in the rough" on it, this means it is in need of repair.

Is the wear in proper places? This is important! Otherwise suspect replacements.

Is the carving on the edges, like gadrooning, all exactly alike? Hand carving will have variations.

Are the edges sharp? Old edges have softened. New replacements can be felt by touching.

Even if not original, brasses should match the period and match the original holes on the piece. Check to see if the original holes have been filled in.

If the original brasses (mounts) survive, carefully removing one will disclose the original finish. This can be very exciting! Mounts were referred to as "brass furniture" by both English Colonial Americans and merchants. Many have engraved catalogue numbers on their reverse side.

If the finish underneath the mount (the brasses) is identical to the outside, it has recently been refinished. If possible, ask to have one brass removed.

The edge of the brass plate will leave a scar on the surface of an old piece.

Early brasses are a light yellow color.

Antique brasses were meant to be kept brightly polished to reflect fire and candlelight.

English brasses, still a part of many fine pieces, can be much larger and more ornate than those made for the American trade. The exception is the brasses used on block and shell pieces made during the Chippendale period in Newport, Rhode Island.

Beautiful William and Mary and Queen Anne highboys have been turned into chests with bracket feet to provide "early chests." If all the parts are genuine, it's almost impossible to spot.

Flat-top, tall pieces have been converted to more valuable scroll-top pieces. A clue is evident in the heavy horizontal board dovetailed into the vertical dividers above the center top drawer. Check the back, behind the questionable area, for splotches of stain.

Pie-crusts can be added to plain topped tables. Always feel the edges. If they feel sharp, look closely. Antique furniture edges look "lived-in."

Table legs were often changed to conform to current tastes. Fine antique pieces had their perfect original legs changed if certain dealers thought they could sell for more money. Crawl underneath and feel for filled in holes. Suggest less money if you still want the piece.

Check feet carefully for damages. Will you have to restore any part of the piece? The price should reflect this.

Anything an old cabinetmaker could do, craftsmen can still do! I repeat, anything an old craftsman could do can still be done!

Old furniture shrinks because wood is 80 to 90 per cent water. It is normal for round tables to be no longer symmetrically round; drawers may no longer fit perfectly; and inlay will show shrinkage.

Early dovetails were not carbon copies of each other, but

later dovetails have identical and uniform shapes. Dovetails can be seen on ancient Egyptian pieces.

Old dowels (wooden pins) are not uniformly round, but those produced by machines are.

Screws were handmade from the sixteenth century through the latter part of the eighteenth century. In 1817, the English invented a thread-cutting machine in which the head was turned and readied for the cut. The concentric ring marks differ from modern screw rings because they look less sharp. Forgers have filed screw heads and threads to make them appear antique.

Old handmade nails were forged, in a furnace, and so are different sizes. They are not uniform. Old nails often bleed on wood around the nail hole.

Early iron nails were squared or triangular.

Eighteenth century nuts are round while hexagonal nuts indicate a later period. It is possible to find new hexagonal nuts on old threads.

New paint, which dents, is not as hard as old paint. Old paint looks softer than new paint and has a mottled patina.

Painted pieces are becoming more important to the collector and are better left alone. It is important not to strip or repaint these pieces since this will destroy their potential value.

England has a long history of grain painting which is the technique of applying paint to imitate the grain of wood.

Do veneered panels, above and below, match? Do they exhibit the same grain patterns?

Dirty furniture looks older than clean furniture, but old dirt and wax build-up in crevices and cracks is a good sign. If pristine, look again.

Check to see if castors have been removed. If so, the value is less. Try to replace with period pieces.

Splotches of stain are a warning. Check the area very carefully, inside and out. Has the area been repaired, remodeled or replaced?

Holes that serve no purpose indicate a substitute piece. Running a small knitting needle underneath the piece can detect such holes. A collector does a lot of crawling under tables.

Don't be afraid to give a little shake to a chair, etagere or hall tree. You want solid, not wiggly furniture. If it is loose, will the dealer see to its repair?

Carry a flashlight and tape measure. Also, keep a notebook for prices, phone numbers, names, etc.

When I hear "there's a piece just like it in the...museum," I wonder. Why am I being offered it? Wouldn't an auction with many potential buyers offer greater rewards? Reproductions are much like museum pieces, while authentic pieces seldom are.

Layers of beeswax contribute to the look and aroma of antiquity. Don't allow "antique perfume" to sway your senses.

Yes, there are forged labels. Labels are easier than ever to produce or reproduce because of new copying equipment and "new grime." Remember to look carefully at the piece and judge on merit.

Old newspapers or memorabilia have been known to find their way into new pieces. This is called salting.

Another reason to check drawers is that sometimes unexpected bonuses have been left in them. I found a collection of very old plaster casts of antique medallions in an old dresser. The dealer had overlooked them and was delighted to part with them for a ridiculously low price.

I have also found, wedged between drawers, old union cards, birth certificates, military documents, letters and post cards. Local historical societies are often grateful to have such items donated, and you are the listed donor.

Up until the Victorian period, English antique chests were made with more than three drawers.

Early chamber or commode chairs have been transformed by removing the deep skirt and replacing the knee brackets. I can't fault this practice.

Short, antique stool legs can be used to construct expensive wing chairs that had short legs. This is why it is preferable to buy an antique frame and have it upholstered.

Love seats can be made from the four legs of an antique chair. The new parts are hidden under the upholstery. If an exposed seat-rail is part of the design, old bed boards can be used.

Oval drop-leaf tables with the leaves too close to the floor may be altered rectangular drop-leaf tables. Since oval drop-leaf tables are more readily sold, oval leaves were substituted to replace existing rectangular leaves. A leaf with two timbers is questionable, as leaves were usually a single piece. If a table reminds you of a basset hound, check the leaves.

Check both sides of a piece because one antique piece can be "twined" to make two antique pieces.

Popular pieces like pine cupboards make me wonder how so many survived. You can be sure that many are new fakes made with some old wood members and a little gesso rubbed on the knots. Put me in the "doubtful column," but I've seen "antiques" with fresh sawdust still clinging.

Sunlight bleaches wood within weeks. Leave a glass paperweight on a piece in direct sunlight and you'll see.

A pile of manure (ammonia) placed near furniture ages it rapidly.

Living insects eat wood exactly like their ancestors (worm holes). Living forgers use ice picks and various sized nails.

A chair with a lion-mask on the knee, made between 1725 and 1745, usually would have a paw foot instead of a claw-and-ball foot.

Although they did not fold into a handsome piece of furniture such as a chair, Georgian library steps were made attractive in themselves.

Georgian breakfronts often were fitted with a desk in the lower central portion.

Various English commodes (circa 1730), show a strong Continental influence. Those with a bombé profile can be identified as French, with the ends of the drawers following the outline of the sides, or English with the drawer's ends cut off square.

Some Hepplewhite dining tables have a rare detail called a serpentine-shaped apron.

An exquisite and unusual Adam detail, found on giltwood and satinwood side tables, is a carved flower filled basket which is centered on the stretcher.

Wedgewood plaques, on pieces like consoles, are another Adam detail.

Victorian drawers are distinguished by the quarter round top of the drawer slips, which are located between the drawer side and the drawer bottom. Typical Victorian drawer construction was one in which the drawer bottom was let into a grooved drawer slip and was pinned or glued on to the drawer side.

Mounts changed with each successive period. Handles and hinges were generally brass, gilded brass, wrought-iron, or the exception—silver.

Hinges on medieval furniture were usually wrought-iron.

Ornamental iron bands are considered mounts.

Elizabethan and Jacobean furniture have iron "H" type hinges, and keys were preferred to handles.

Post-Restoration brass replaced iron, and handles became increasingly decorative. Silver mounts that were embossed and chased are found on various marquetry pieces, including corner plates, escutcheons and handles.

Brass was the most popular mount.

In the late seventeenth and eighteenth centuries, drop handles in pear or acorn design hung from a circular plate with the escutcheon in a cartouche shape.

Early Georgian mounts had a loop mounted on a shaped plate. A bail pull, on a brass plate, with a convex center curve is called a "swan's-neck" mount or handle.

Later mounts had cutout plates giving a scroll or strapwork design. Some were called open-fret plates.

Eighteenth century plates used "roses" or rosettes.

Adam plates were often of oval shape with loops.

Nineteenth century mounts were often of a lion-mask with a ring.

Victorian mounts were often cast from molds and easily reproduced. Cheap loops were also used.

TIMBER LINES

Wood is our basic furniture material.

The identification of woods is not always an easy task; museums often have a question mark in their card files. The basic English woods, oak, walnut, satinwood and rosewood, usually do not present a problem.

In the eighteenth century, while Virginia walnut was sent to England, English plank oak was being sent to Maryland in America.

After the Revolutionary War, American Tories brought American-made furniture back to England. Much of this furniture came from New York where copied English furniture closely and clearly reflected the dominance of the Loyalists in the city's population. Examples of this antique American furniture can be found at the American Museum in Bath, England, which has one of the world's finest collections of antique American furniture.

Wood alone will seldom determine origin.

A natural patina, which is the furniture surface, should be even in color and have a mellow quality.

Old wood develops soft, warm color hues. The surface of a piece changes naturally with time.

Wood colors change gradually from exposure to light, and to polishes used on it. The raised portion of carved ornaments will be lighter from rubbing while recessed portions of carving will be darker from wax build-up and dirt that has lodged in the crevices.

French polishing began in the Victorian period. This type of polishing resulted in a high glass-like finish. It took a shorter time to achieve than the previous spirit varnish and oil and wax polishes of the seventeenth and eighteenth centuries, whose application required considerable more time and labor. However, French polishing harmed many earlier pieces when applied because it destroyed the original patina.

Poorly restored pieces will appear harsh compared with naturally aged antiqued pieces.

Splotches of stain indicate a patina is not natural. Look for repairs, restoration or replacements. Check the inside of a casepiece as carefully as the outside.

Do not strip an old piece unless there is no other way to restore it. Many furniture refinishers have no soul and less sense and want to charge you for a refinishing job. Explore every alternative first. The beauty as well as the value of the piece will suffer greatly if the natural patina is totally removed. *Antique furniture should not look like new.*

Old timbers can be extremely wide (old mahogany trees produced timbers twelve feet wide) and are not uniform in width.

Timbers are strongest along the grain.

Backboards on antique casepieces were made of random widths.

Wood-burning fireplaces and later coal fires darkened wood tones.

Furniture pests still invade furniture. They can eat an arm or leg until the member eventually cracks and a grayish powder spills out (dry rot). An expert must clean out the diseased area and fill it in or replace the part. Some refinishing is usually proper and necessary. Check cracks carefully.

Veneer is a thin layer of wood applied over a base wood or carcass.

Marquetry is actually a sophisticated form of veneering.

Marquetry with ivory, dyed woods or bone, are likely to be Continental rather than English or American.

For inlay and marquetry the English used various woods such as holly, sycamore, yew, satinwood, calamander, stained pear, ebony, bog oak and olive.

The English used woods such as walnut, zebra, purplewood, kingwood, anboyna and acacia for banding.

Plywood on the underframing of a carcass base indicates recent repair.

Old hand cut veneers can be nearly $1/8$ of an inch thick. Since 1840, machine cut veneers are $1/32$ to $1/64$ of an inch thick. Newer veneers hold more securely because glues hold the thinner veneers tighter. Animal glues were used on antique pieces. Today many synthetic polyvinyl resin adhesives are employed.

Crotch-grain means veneer generally cut from the main crotch or fork of a tree.

Burl (burr) veneer is the growth from a tree sliced and glued to a wood base.

Oyster piece is the name for a type of veneer derived by transverse slices (cross-direction) of a bough or root to form concentric circles. Walnut and laburnum made wonderful oyster veneers in the seventeenth century along with yew, elm and mulberry.

Figures are timber designs brought out by cutting the wood so veneers or solid surfaces display various types of irregularities in the grain and color.

Old English oak has a coarse, raised grain that you can feel with your fingertips.

American oak can retain its golden color while English oak usually darkens.

Oak resembles chestnut and ash which all have distinct pores. Chestnut, however, does not have the rays that oak has.

Walnut, mahogany and satinwood darken with age unless faded from the sun.

Walnut grays from sunlight.

Walnut timbers may produce markings of stripes, waves and mottles.

European walnut has a finer grain than American walnut.

American walnut was used for English furniture from about 1720. This was because English forests had thinned and because English walnut had more knots and was more susceptible to furniture insects. The American variety may be darker in tone.

Victorian black walnut was created by applying a stain or acid to walnut tinged with red, and then was stained very dark.

Mahogany is called the perfect cabinet wood.

Mahogany does not gray from sunlight.

Mahogany has plain figures and swirl grains. The timbers may show striped dark elliptical markings referred to as "plum pudding."

Fiddle-back figures are primarily found on Honduras mahogany.

More mahogany pieces have survived in better shape than

walnut ones because walnut pieces were often veneered. I have seen old veneered pieces that show more of the base wood than remaining pieces of veneer. They look naked.

Santo Domingo mahogany pieces develop an exquisite patina over a long time. If stripped, remember that they will require another hundred years to regain their true beauty.

Spanish and Cuban mahogany handled sunlight better than the Honduras variety which lightened considerably.

A dark mahogany piece was probably polished with oil as polishing with wax results in a lighter tone.

What constitutes proper care of furniture? Concerning humidity, if you are comfortable, your furniture will also be comfortable. What about waxing? Wax not more than twice a year with a fine paste wax. No sprays and liquids! Dust with a soft cloth. When cleaning, do not bump or damage your pieces. Do not leave any porous clay or pottery pots with plants or flowers on your furniture. If you do these simple things, your antique pieces will look beautiful.

WOODS

The five major woods used on English furniture were:

Oak The primary wood used in England throughout the Middle Ages until the mid-seventeenth century. Important again for Arts and Crafts pieces in the Victorian period.

Walnut Grown in England from the mid-seventeenth century, walnut was used for the furniture made during the Tudor period. It is browner than mahogany, and has timber markings of stripe and mottle. Irregular growths, crooks, forks, stumps and burls (burr) produced prized veneers. It is a carving wood.

Mahogany Beginning in the sixteenth century it was used for ship building. A strong tropical wood (perhaps the best came from Cuba), mahogany is known as the ideal cabinet and fine carving wood. It has a variety of figures and takes a fine polish. The color ranges from yellowish or pinkish tones to deep reddish or purplish brown. Mahogany does not gray from sunlight. Chippendale made extremely fine pieces from this wood.

Satinwood Imported from the West and East Indies. It is of a yellow color and can be used solid or as veneer. Many satinwood pieces were designed by Robert Adam in the latter part of the eighteenth century.

Rosewood Imported from Brazil. Light brown to deep red tones, and is strongly marked but with an even grain. May have streaks. Important in the Regency period.

Country pieces were made from various local woods.

Other woods used were:

Acacia   Yellow wood with brown markings, used for eighteenth century bandings.

Amboyna   Native to the West Indies, has a bird's-eye figure of golden brown color. Used in the late eighteenth century for banding and marquetry.

Applewood   Light reddish-brown, close-grained. Used in the seventeenth century as a veneer and for inlay.

Ash   Tree native to Britain. Grayish-white to pale yellow. Used for the back-rail of Windsor chairs in the eighteenth century.

Birch   Tree native to Britain. Wood has a pale, yellowish tint when polished. Can be stained to resemble maple, cherry, mahogany and walnut. It is used as a cheap substitute for satinwood.

Bog Oak   Black in color. Used for inlay on Elizabethan and Jacobean furniture.

Boxwood   Yellow, without figure; fine grain. From the sixteenth century for inlay on oak, and walnut and satinwood in the eighteenth century.

Calamander   Imported from Ceylon and in use from 1780 for decorative veneer work. A mottled brown with black streaks.

Cedar   Imported from North America and the West Indies. Often used for pieces like tables as well as linings.

Cherry   Reddish, close-grained wood used in the seventeenth century for inlay.

Cypress   Reddish colored wood, close-grained, hard and durable. Popular for chests, especially in the sixteenth and seventeenth centuries.

Ebony Black wood. Chiefly used for decorative treatment, inlay and marquetry. Many Anglo-Indian pieces were made of solid ebony.

Elm Hard wood used for chairs and tables in Tudor times and for Windsor chairs in the Georgian period. Also important in the Victorian period.

Fir Used in the eighteenth century for carved and gilded parts of highly decorative tables.

Kingwood Decorative wood from Brazil. First appeared in England in the late eighteenth century. Used for crossbanding.

Lignum Vitae From West Indies, with a dark brown and black streaky figure. Used in the seventeenth century for veneer and also solid.

Limewood Very popular for decorative carved work due to its fine white grain. Examples are found in the late seventeenth century when Grinling Gibbons made exceptional limewood carvings.

Olive A greenish-yellow with black veining and spots. Used in the seventeenth century for parquetry.

Pear Light brown; no figure. Often stained black as a less expensive alternative to ebony.

Pine Conifer The timber usually called deal. Used for drawers and later for cheap furniture.

Plywood Layers of wood glued over each other. Plywood has been used for centuries.

Purplewood From Brazil. The purple changes to brown on exposure. Used for bandings on eighteenth century furniture.

Sycamore Very fine grain, yellowish-white, used in veneer in floral marquetry during the seventeenth century. Later stained a green-gray, it was called harewood.

Thuja Imported from Africa. Rich brown color, with a bird's-eye figure. Sometimes used as a veneer in the early eighteenth century.

Tulip A soft, light wood. A secondary wood, often used for painted pieces.

White maple Used from the seventeenth century for marquetry.

Yew A reddish-brown, hard and springy wood. Used from sixteenth century for furniture. Used for construction parts, veneer and Windsor chairs.

Zebra wood Imported from South America. Strongly streaked in light and dark brown. Used for veneer and cross-banding. Examples found on Regency pieces.

AUCTION TERMS
(More under Selling and Buying)

An auction is a public sale where property goes to the highest bidder.

Today we have a global auction market. Market value is similar the world over.

The auction house owns no property; it is the agent providing a service to the seller and buyer.

Services can be negotiated!

Larger auction houses have separate departments for furniture, paintings, etc. Each department has an expert in charge, produces catalogues and handles sales. You can write or phone an auction house requesting particular catalogues or particular sale information. There is a charge for catalogues, but you can get them either on an individual or a subscription basis. You can request price (digests) sheets listing what each particular piece in the sale sold for. There is also a charge for this service.

Auction viewing rooms are a good place to see, handle and learn about furniture. Treat yourself to hours of pleasure before the sale in a category you are most interested in.

The private collector has the edge over the dealer who must buy at a price that enables him to sell at a profit.

The commission to the auction house is called a "buyer's premium."

There is also a "seller's premium."

An absentee or pocket bid is an offer given in person, or by mail, to the auctioneer before the sale. The record of absentee bids is kept by the house and given the same recognition as bids made during the actual sale. The record of an absentee bid is termed "book."

Be sure you know what the piece you bid on looks like and take notes when you view it. The house will allow you to handle the piece under supervision before the sale at a "viewing time." Note distinguishing marks, cracks, colors, scratches, etc.

A "switch" is the substitution of a piece originally on view, for one of a lower value prior to or after the sale.

If you cannot be present at a particular auction and are hesitant to offer an absentee bid without viewing the piece or pieces, many dealers will bid for you. They should agree to phone you after examining the object to describe the condition. Then, if you wish, to bid for you on an agreed-on price. You will pay a commission to the dealer in addition to the one you pay the house. Only contact dealers that handle this particular type of object and who will be attending the auction to buy for themselves. You do not want a dealer who is not familiar with the type of piece you plan to bid on.

"As is" is an auction term meaning the article is some way damaged and will be sold in that condition.

A "reserve" is the lowest price agreed on by the seller and the house beneath which the article cannot be sold. The seller will take the article back if that price is not reached.

An "unreserved auction" means there is no reserve and the article goes to the highest bidder no matter how low the last bid is.

A "hidden reserve" is a reserve agreed upon by the seller and the house, unknown to the bidder.

Auction catalogues often give an estimate for each item. Example: $1,000 to $1,500. *The $1,000 is not the reserve.* If you want to leave an absentee bid, perhaps offer 70 per cent of the low or $700.

"Chandelier bids" or "phantom bids" are false bids used by auctioneers to increase genuine bidding at sales.

A "pool" is a clutch of bidders, not necessarily dealers, who attempt to restrain or force up bidding for their personal profit.

A "ring" is a group, usually dealers, who gather together to cheat the house and the seller by keeping the bidding (if possible) between themselves, and keeping it low. The "ring" after acquiring said object or objects may then hold another auction among themselves to divide the goodies.

Do not pass up auctions which don't specialize in the furniture you collect. You may find just what you are searching for, at a reasonable price, hidden among the featured furniture. For example, if you collect Regency furniture, attending an auction billed as featuring "Country English," there may be an isolated Regency piece available at a price much less than would be the case if other Regency collectors were bidding against you.

Call an auction house after a sale to see if unsold pieces are available below the original reserve. You would still be responsible for the auction house commission. Individual auction house policies would dictate any possible procedure. The owner of any piece in question would have to be consulted and agree before a post-auction sale.

CLARIFICATIONS

Authentic furniture has its origin supported by unquestionable evidence.

A reproduction or replica is a copy. With a little help it might be sold as an authentic piece.

A fake is a copy of an authentic piece made to be sold as if it were the "real thing." "Nice people" sell "unnice" pieces.

Repairs. This term refers to small mending, not substituting or adding new parts to any degree.

Restoration is more than simple repair. It means to renew and return a piece to its original state. New parts can be substituted for missing or damaged ones. *Restoration is proper and important.* A major restoration is the replacement of front legs, the feet, case-piece tops, one or more drawers; reshaping a seat frame, a chair splat, the wings of an armchair, and similar work. Without restoration, many lovely pieces would be lost forever. Therefore, skilled crafts people are very valuable and expert workmanship is very important.

"Subbed" or "monkeyed" is substituting parts, or making a repair or addition, such as a carved shell, for the purpose of making a piece look older or more valuable.

Natural patina is a mellow quality that furniture surfaces acquire with age.

Unnatural patina. A wood surface showing the result of refinishing, French polishing or other unnatural devices.

A "divorce" is separating a piece into two parts. This is done when the parts are worth more separate than the original piece as a whole.

What about married pieces? They are two pieces not originally designed together but may be combined. Example: a chest and a bookcase. Married furniture can be desirable if it is properly identified.

Transitional furniture is furniture with details from two

contiguous periods. This is why it is important to know the major periods and the order in which they appear. The latest characteristics on a piece determine its period.

An appraisal is the worth of a piece valued by an expert. It is usually in writing, and often used for insurance purposes.

Market value is the retail cash value of a piece.

Provenance is a written history or pedigree of a piece—who originally owned it, where it was made, when last sold, and so on.

TUDOR AND EARLY STUART 1485-1600

We can visualize the history of English furniture in various ways. The first might be to separate the periods: Tudor, Stuart, early Georgian, late Georgian, Regency and Victorian. Or we might commence with early Medieval, to Renaissance, to Baroque, to Rococo, to Neo-Classicism, to diversity and on to aestheticism. We could also study English furniture using the "ages" of oak, walnut, mahogany, satinwood and rosewood. We might arrange a furniture chart listing rulers, architecture or even design elements. Which ever path we choose, the first piece encountered would be the basic medieval storage chest.

Prior to and during the sixteenth century, early Tudor furniture was made by arkwrights. Chests were called arks, or coffers, and were usually made of oak (walnut was not used during this early period). The first chests (chists) were hollowed out logs, with an occasional lid made from the same log. The next stage was a chest constructed of four boards with a bottom and a lid. These primitive pieces were multi-purposed. They stored possessions, were sat upon, slept on, or served as a table. From the tenth to the twelfth century, chests were decorated with chip carving, gouge carving, punch work and paint. The designs were often geometric and iron parts used to reinforce chests also became a decoration. Iron work progressed to become an art form of the smiths.

In the 1200s, furniture was constructed with turned elements, butt joints, and mortice and tenon joints which were anchored with crude clout-headed nails. Then, in the 1300s, mortice and tenon joints secured by dowels became common and dovetail joints evolved. Iron bands held planks firmly together and were also decorative.

Joined chests were in existence from the thirteenth century. Broad vertical stiles began from the lid and continued on to form the feet of the chest. The stiles framed the boards which made up the front and the back. The lid was a single board and was attached with pin-hinges. Joints were fixed by dowel pegs. The front and back were tenonned into the stiles.

Extra strength was sometimes achieved by the draw-bore practice, where the pinhole through the tenon was made slightly out of line with those in the mortice wall so that as the dowel pin was hammered in, it tightened the tenon. The expression "a square peg in a round hole" comes from this method of joining furniture elements. Green wood was used for the pegs. Contrary to how we use this expression today, the draw-bore method worked.

If decorated, the designs were composed of roundels, geometric patterns, interlaced foliage, arches or grooved borders. Near the end of the fifteenth century, chests had iron hinges. By the fifteenth century, panel furniture (architectural funiture) with mortice and tenon joints prevailed. After the fifteenth century, various linen-fold patterns and Renaissance designs were used. (Panelled framing of chest fronts was usual before the sixteenth century.)

Medieval folks used rough pieces made by an arkwright or by a huchier. The huchier's limited ability extended to constructing chests (arks) or primitive cupboards or hutches (hence the name). These crude, early hutches were actually an extra broad chest made of oak planks with a pivot-hinged door, held together with large clout-headed nails.

The ambry was a cupboard which could be free-standing or could be built into an existing wall. Those with pierced doors were usually for food storage.

Four legged, turned stools were common in the twelfth century. However, chests were more important in these early times and continue to be in use to the present day.

The typical Tudor chair was heavy, with a tall straight back, solid arms support and was a box form. The space below the seat was for storage. Panelled joined chairs with turned legs, stretchers, and open arms appear in the latter half of the sixteenth century. They were often embellished with the owner's initials and dated. The Gothic style of carving and decoration grew bolder by the close of the fifteenth century. Designs of geometrics, lunettes, intertwined shapes, arches, leaves and flowers were carved on these early chairs.

By the close of the sixteenth century, there were three singular types of chairs produced by three separate craftsmen. The first was the joiners box or panel chair. The second was the "thrown" chair which developed from the stool and was made by a turner. The third was the very rare upholstered chair with a joiner-made frame.

The framed table was introduced about the middle of the sixteenth century and continued to be made throughout the Stuart period. This table had heavy turned legs and outside stretcher rails. They were made of oak, walnut, ash and elm. Since elm is a perishable wood, tables made of it rarely survive. These tables were constructed with four, six or eight legs and their tops overhang the carcass.

The draw-top table had additional leaves that could be extended out at each end. When not needed they remained under the main board which composed the top.

Other early seventeenth century pieces were the court and press cupboards. The court cupboard, generally the smaller of the two, was used to display plates, flagons and cups which showed the wealth of the owner. The press cupboards were for food storage. Court cupboards of oak, inlaid with sycamore and bog oak, with all-over carving, and turned balusters flanking the top portion with a central door, are impressive pieces. Early cupboards always were designed with a central door. Double doors indicate a later time-frame. A late Gothic oak ambry (a court cupboard) might have doors with simple carving and pierced roundels. An oak press might have front carved recessed panels decorated with geometric shapes. Cupboards were decorated with ebonized moldings, carved pine decorations, carved foliage, lozenges, or carved leaves and berries.

The oak clothes press or wardrobe appears in the seventeenth century. Early press cupboards, also called livery cupboards, had closed storage at the top and a shelf in the lower section. These were two tiered pieces, usually with a shelf at the lowest level. Livery cupboards might have a pot shelf at the bottom. These pieces were carved with geometric, arched, intertwining, panel and foliate designs. Both court and livery pieces were often painted.

Painted furniture has a long history in the English furniture tradition. There is written evidence, found in early letters and bills, like "one payntyed table for cups," "a rede coffer," and "a bedstead paynted green." (Note the spellings of "painted.") Marbleizing, lacquering and speckling are employed in later periods.

Some pieces were left untreated, but later in the period they were coated with beeswax for preservation. Sadly, early pieces with original patina are scarce. The English thought nothing of stripping their old pieces. It wasn't until 1830 when the practice of refinishing old furniture began in earnest.

The union of England and Scotland in 1603, under James I, was symbolized by the rose and thistle. James I furniture is called Jacobean. It echoed elements of Elizabeth I, having, besides the rose and thistle, bulbous supports, carved foliage scrolls, fluting and strapwork. Tulips flanked by hearts are found on cane chairs and winged heads appear on late sixteenth century chests.

In 1660, when Charles II returned from exile, carvings became more lavish with pulsating curves and more lush foliage. Various motifs were carved on these medieval pieces. The fleur-de-lis dates to England's former claim to France, surrendered in 1559 by Elizabeth I. About 1660, designs included vine and bird, and a favorite flower was the carnation.

LATE STUART 1600-1700

The late Stuart period began with optimism when Charles II was restored to the throne. The Great Fire of London, in 1656, had destroyed tremendous amounts of furniture and many lumber yards. When people were able to replace lost furniture, they wanted a change. They turned to walnut rather than their previous favorite, oak. Carved elements and furniture designs blossomed with fuller outlines. Foreign influences began to make inroads on traditional designs. French and Dutch immigrants contributed their heritage with veneering, marquetry, parquetry, japanning, gesso and spiral twists. In the 1680s, French Huguenot metal workers immigrated to Britain and brought wonderful exciting designs to the existing blacksmithing trades.

Floral marquetry, a Dutch contribution, was an exuberant form of inlay. This was different from traditional inlay of colorful woods placed into the surface of a piece. Marquetry was a total overlay of veneer onto the carcass that formed a separate wood layer.

New pieces appear at this time. A very important piece was the chest of drawers which offered great convenience in contrast to the basic chest. Gate-leg tables were also a new piece. When extended they could be round, oval or polygonal (having three or more straight sides). They had from three to twelve supports, were joined by mortice and tenon, and secured with dowel pins. Now long tables were not fashionable as people desired small intimate tables. Many of these early smaller tables made of oak, walnut, yew and fruitwoods still exist.

Special shops handle furniture from this period and occasionally some pieces come up for auction.

After 1615, the "back-stool" made its appearance. The back was a rectangular pad attached horizontally between the back stiles. The seat was a stool form. This produced a simple chair with no arms. The openings between the back pad and the seat allowed women wearing a farthingale (a hoop skirt) to sit comfortably. These "back-stools" became the "farthingale chair" and originally were considered a women's chair. This style was subsequently used for dining, in which case it might have had a leather back pad and leather seat. The design took another form when it was made as a Great Chair. It was enlarged, had its seat raised, acquired arms, was upholstered in velvet and given a foot stool. It was no longer a women's chair.

"X"-frame chairs, originally a Roman design, were favored as seats of authority. Leaders of the period were often portrayed in engravings and paintings seated in these chairs. The subjects were painted in great finery; the chairs were shown upholstered in velvet, finely fringed and decorated with brass tacks.

The English "sleeping chair" had a hinged back adjusted by means of iron hatchets. It permitted sleep in a sitting position. It was also one of the earliest types of flexible chairs with a moving part.

There is no evidence that rush-bottomed chairs were made in England before 1700. However, it is probable that this type of chair was produced earlier because it had appeared long before in other contexts such as baskets.

Wicker chairs were common in bed chambers for invalids and women. These chairs had squabs (cushions) which were added for comfort.

Sofas were not a common piece before 1700, but some "sophas" were already old by this time. An English sofa of the 1690s was formed like two adjacent easy chairs and often had gilded legs. Others had a headboard type back that is more like those we are accustomed to seeing today.

Veneered cabinet pieces were made with solid walnut or walnut veneer. Veneering consisted of thin slices of wood glued on the surface of the furniture carcass. The cuts of these slices had rich decorative figures and fancy grains.

Oriental lacquered furniture was imported by the East India Company around 1660. This form of decoration was deemed very fashionable and desirable. The term "Japann" was applied to actual Oriental pieces as well as pieces made in England. English japanning was achieved by building up a ground of whiting (crushed chalk) to which many coats of varnish were applied and then decorated with gilded designs. Black was the most used ground color; red was rather unusual; tortoise-shell was achieved by combining red and black; and white or blue japanning was rare.

Early japanned pieces had no cornices. Some japanned cabinets were made in Holland or the Orient, and placed on English stands that were richly carved. Later, during the Queen Anne period, cornices became elaborate, and in the William and Mary period there were a variety of pediments.

Twisted, spiral turnings were not made from brittle oak, but from walnut or beech. Originally, they were cut by hand, but after 1660 twisting was accomplished by a slide rest on a lathe. These spiral turnings were often used on cane chairs, open armchairs with upholstery, cabinet stands, gate-leg tables and rest beds.

Chair designs of this period, commonly associated with "William and Mary," were upholstered or caned, had scrolled legs joined by a large scrollwork front stretcher, curved arms and curvilinear flat stretchers. Some were made of walnut while others were painted and gilded. Others had curved "X" stretchers. The legs on William and Mary furniture had a variety of shapes. Some of the legs were scrolled, some were baluster-turned, some geometrically or cup-turned, or had inverted cup turnings. The feet were predominantly scroll, and were called Spanish or Braganza.

QUEEN ANNE AND EARLY GEORGIAN 1702-1740

Queen Anne furniture was elegant and restrained. English furniture, for the first time, had curves that followed the human shape. Domestic comfort was given consideration. Graceful cabriole legs did not need stretchers as did earlier heavy legs. Stuffed upholstery was replaced by drop seats. Seat backs assumed a curve, and the center of the chair back had a central solid splat. The seat-rail also curved. The now important cabriole leg (an Oriental design) had various feet such as the Dutch pad, ribbed, snake, slipper, and paw or hoof foot. Later in the period, the ball-and-claw foot appeared. Carved decoration was simple and usually confined to the knees of cabriole legs, crest-rails, seat-rails and aprons.

The major design element of this period's furniture was a shell that can be traced directly to the Dutch escallop. Carved masks were sometimes carved on the seat-rail of chairs.

In the early part of the period, fine figured walnut was the predominant wood, but mahogany later became the favorite. In the transitional span between walnut and mahogany, the elegant and graceful Queen Anne hooped-back changed to a ponderous awkward chair. Mid-Georgian furniture, in the meantime, took on Rococo characteristics.

The upholstered wing chair, with the wings at the shoulder curved down to the padded out-scrolled arms, cabriole legs and stretchers for the extra weight, was a lovely and comfortable furniture addition.

Typical Queen Anne arms were shaped in a continuous curve. Love seats or double seats became in vogue. As the period evolved, chair splats became ornate with gilding, marquetry and japanning.

The bureau-desk with bracket feet, the charming tea table, the bureau-bookcase, and the card or game table with counter wells (guinea pockets) and candle recesses, were exquisite new furniture pieces. Lowboys often had cross-banded borders. Drop-leaf tables had cabriole legs and pad feet. Kneehole desks with cross-banded tops, in burr walnut with bracket feet, were similar to earlier William and Mary pieces but did not have marquetry. The Windsor chair also made its appearance during this period.

Writing cabinets were constructed in two stages. The upper part of this cabinet piece had a double hood with three finials. The doors in the upper part were inset with mirror glass and enclosed a fitted interior of small drawers and pigeon holes. The top drawer of the lower portion was closed by a flap that formed a writing surface and was supported by slides. This piece had ball feet, tear-drop brasses and brass escutcheons. It might also have herringbone cross-banding.

Another piece was a cabinet-on-chest with a moulded cornice. These pieces, chests-on-chests and tallboys often had large cavetto mouldings on their cornices. Some cabinets had a single hood or dome while others had double hoods or domes. Bow-front hanging corner cabinets were important in veneered walnut.

Lacquered pieces were in brilliant colors such as vermillion and emerald green. Gilding continued in vogue.

During the reign of George I, furniture continued in the Queen Anne design but was of heavier construction. Castors (originally spelled "casters") began to be used on chair and table feet. The eagle's head with the beak turned outward appeared on chair arms. The hairy paw foot and the ball-and-claw foot dominated Georgian legs. The open splat with narrow vertical cuts became popular. The lion and satyr mask became a distinguishing motif on the knees of cabriole legs. Winged satyrs emerged on knees and chair-rails, and cabochons and leaf carving also decorated knees.

The cabinetmakers of the early Georgian period whose workshops produced fine quality furniture were John Coxed and T. Woster during the reign of Queen Anne; John Gumley and James Moore in the time of George I; Benjamin Goodison, William Hallet and Giles Grendey, who was known for his japanned pieces.

MID-GEORGIAN OR ROCOCO 1740-1765

The mid-Georgian period had three major influences: Rococo, Chinese and Gothic. The Rococo style consisted of ornate decoration using foliage, shells, scrolls and whorls. Chinese designs were a revival of earlier chinoiserie motifs, although now this influence took the form of pagodas, lattice-work, and open and blind fret-work. Chinese wallpapers were highly prized. The major characteristic of Gothic was the pointed (lancet) arch. Gothic Revival cannot be mentioned without discussing Horace Walpole and the Strawberry Hill house he transformed into a famous Gothic villa.

Pattern and design books were published during this time. They were produced by architects, builders and artists, but not by craftsmen. The one exception was the stellar publication of Thomas Chippendale called the *Director*. (The full title is *Gentlemen and Cabinet-Maker's Director*.) It was the first pattern book devoted entirely to furniture and the first to be published by a cabinetmaker and master carver. Sixty-five per cent of the initial subscribers to the *Director* were furniture-related craftsmen, not the gentry.

Chippendale's designs were so widely followed that a whole general category of eighteenth century furniture is commonly grouped under his name. Chippendale and Rococo style became interchangeable. He included French, Oriental and Gothic elements. Chippendale was not the only designer to interpret Chinese designs. Matthew Darly and George Edwards published *A New Book of Chinese Designs* that also inspired many adaptions. Some of Chippendale's most important work was in Neo-Classic designs, but that will not come until the late Georgian period.

Early in his career, Chippendale built on earlier Queen Anne designs. He replaced the solid Queen Anne splat with pierced carved splats. These had designs of arches, ruffles, loops, hearts, reverse curves, diamonds, ribbons and tassels. Pendant husks, trefoils, quatrefoils and Chinese lattice were also used for the splat. The cabriole leg with a claw-and-ball foot or Dutch pad foot was used on the open splat chair.

The open-work splat on Chippendale chairs had a French origin. A perfect example is the Chippendale ribbon-back chair, with cabriole legs terminating in a French whorl or scroll foot. His crest-rails flattened the Queen Anne curve and became serpentine. They were referred to as a cupid's bow shape. Due to the strength of mahogany, it was an exceptional wood for carving. Now it was possible to create exciting complex designs on the open-work splats. Perhaps his most celebrated chair backs are the "ribboned-backs," which had interlaced carved ribbons. A knotted or interlaced ribbon, sometimes with a tassel and cord displayed the Rococo character of these masterpieces. The legs were cabriole or straight and stretchered.

Chippendale also designed Chinese-influenced chairs. Some had backs composed of lattice-work, others a pagoda on the crest-rail, usually with straight squared legs with fret-work. (Fretwork that covers wood and cannot be seen through is called "blind fret.") He also used fret brackets between the seat-rail and the legs.

Chippendale used Gothic details like tall arches, carved pinnacles and trefoils on furniture such as chairs, tables and bookcases. His Gothic chairs had lancet arches in the center splat, or the entire back was composed of these arch forms. Gothic designs will reemerge in the Victorian period. The *Director* also has examples of "French style" upholstered armchairs. Chippendale style included many existing designs.

After 1730, cabriole legs were shorter, feet were scrolled, knees were often leaf carved, seat-rails gadrooned, and the seats tapered from front to back. Cabochons were used more extensively on knees.

Another chair, attributed to Chippendale, was the ladder-back. Perhaps of Dutch origin, this design had been in use for a long time, but Chippendale refined and developed it. His first version had cross-rails between the uprights in a wavy line that followed the crest-rail. The cross-rails were also made in an open-work design.

Chippendale designed many upholstered armchairs. The wood portions of these chairs, the seat-rail and legs, display fine foliated Rococo carving. Chippendale specialized in "love seats" also called "Darby and Joan seats" which were actually double chairs.

Many chests of drawers, referred to as "commodes," displayed a French influence and were very elaborate. Chests were also in Chinese taste. After 1750, higher chests featuring five or six drawers were fashionable. These taller chests had mahogany veneers and carving on their friezes, corners, feet and drawer fronts. Various chests had serpentine japanned fronts and carving on their canted corners.

Mahogany was the wood of choice for the typical dining table. The design was two central pieces with wide flaps on either side, and two semi-circular end pieces, all four joined by brass clips. Four cabriole legs supported the larger pieces and two legs supported the smaller ones.

Cards were a popular pastime in Georgian society and many tables were made for this purpose. These tables had counter wells and many were dished to hold candles. Some had candle-brackets which swung from the frieze. These tables displayed beautiful carving on the knee and frieze, often the edges were gadrooned and most were made of mahogany.

Gothic designs in the mid-Georgian period were very different from those of the Medieval period. Furniture forms were not Gothic in shape, but Gothic decorations were important. An example would be the variety of Gothic designs of glazing bars on glass front secretary doors and bookcases. The chair back with arches was made by many designers, not just Chippendale. These Gothic Revival type chairs were often made with cabriole legs and claw-and-ball feet. Gothic designs were often used in dining rooms and in halls. Gothic designs reemerged as revival pieces in the Victorian period.

Another important table was the tripod with claw-and-ball, Dutch or scroll feet. They often had galleries that were fretted or scalloped.

Large library tables made of mahogany with carved mouldings and often enriched with gilding, were in demand. Chippendale had eleven designs for library tables in his third edition of the *Director*, including Rococo, Chinese and Gothic designs.

By the 1760s Chinese designs were passé and new ideas were emerging. The cabriole leg was giving way to a newer, straighter one. Robert Adam, the architect and designer, was introducing the Neo-Classical style. Adam would revive inlay work, emphasize corner pilasters, ovals, dentil designs, key designs and make use of classical mythological figures.

Other designers of this period who should be mentioned are: John Mayhew, William Ince, William Linnell, William Vile and John Cobb, William Hallett and Benjamin Goodison.

LATE GEORGIAN 1765-1800

In this period, earlier Rococo designs with their voluptuous curves were exchanged for the rather austere designs associated with the Classical period. Neo-Classical furniture design was tied to the architecture of the home and it reached a pinnacle of beauty and craftsmanship in the late Georgian period. Three designers in particular are associated with these years: Adam, Hepplewhite and Sheraton. Adam designed for wealthy English patrons, yet his style never became a presence in America. Hepplewhite and Sheraton produced furniture manuals that were extremely important to the American craftsman as well as to the English. Strangely, Hepplewhite did not enjoy the reputation in England that Chippendale did, and Sheraton died in poverty. (The firms of Gillow, Seddon, Ince and Mayhew were widely regarded throughout this period and conducted more lucrative businesses than did Hepplewhite and Sheraton.)

While the furniture designs of Adam were replacing those of Chippendale, Chippendale was still hard at work—some of his finest furniture was created in his later years. He supplied cabinet work to Nostell Priory, and produced pieces for Harewood House in Yorkshire. He was patronized by Sir Edward Knatchbull, and sent work to Kent, Badmonton. He also furnished Garrick's house at Hampton, Alnwich.

Classical ornament had appealed to various architects and designers from the early eighteenth century, but Robert Adam, with his friend, James Stuart, introduced this lighter style. They were inspired by the designs of ancient Greece and Rome, and the discovery and excavations of Herculaneum and Pompeii in Italy.

Robert Adam considered the house and its furnishings as a consistent whole. The cabriole leg, so long important, was replaced with a straight tapered leg. Crest-rails were molded in a more delicate fashion. Seats shrunk and backs were lowered, as ladies' clothing became less voluminous. (Adam also designed chairs with cane seats.)

The motifs Adam favored were delicately handled winged griffins, vases draped with loopings of husks, ribbons, leaves, ovals (patera), honeysuckles, rams' heads, medallions, acanthus leaves and plaques depicting classical subjects. He worked in fine inlay and low relief carving. He used fluting and channeling on furniture backs, arms and legs. Satinwood was used as a veneer and in solid form. Many pieces were gilded or painted as an alternative to inlay. Beechwood was employed if furniture was to be gilded; holly, ebony and tulip woods were used for inlay.

The sideboard was a late eighteenth century design for which Adam is given credit.

Adam and his brothers, John, James and William were all trained architects as was their father, William.

George Hepplewhite was influenced by the designs of Robert Adam. His pieces are delicate and graceful with curvilinear forms. He was most famous for his shield-back chair design which have distinctive backs shaped with entwined hearts, intertwined ovals, lyre designs, ovals with open-work, splats (consisting of narrow curving bars which terminate in a carved wheat design), and banisters. He also designed a square-backed chair that he sometimes upholstered. His legs are usually tapered, plain, fluted or reeded, and often have a delicate spade foot which was often carved. Stretchers are usually absent unless the piece has squared legs.

Pier tables were among the more decorative of Hepplewhite's pieces, having beautiful inlays executed in a variety of woods including white holly. His secretary (secretaire) bookcases are graceful with French feet, curved aprons and glazed doors. The face of the upper drawer is lowered by means of a spring and quadrant.

Hepplewhite sofas carried on the Chippendale influence, but later pieces had an arched top-rail that terminated in a downward curve.

In armchairs, the arm and arm supports usually followed one continuous sweep.

Hepplewhite maintained Adam's sideboard design, but is credited with serpentine and bow-fronted shapes. These pieces have four front legs, and two at the rear that are tapered or squared and end in a plain foot. These rectangular pieces consist of a central drawer flanked by a pair of lateral cupboards or deep wine drawers. Narrow cross-banding appears on the edges, alternating dark and light stringing and inlay of shell and patera, and flowers decorate these pieces.

Another piece associated with Hepplewhite was a semicircular commode (demi-lune) designed in satinwood with rich inlay. It has four projecting columns extending through the body which separated the storage space into three compartments, each with drawers. The end pieces are triangular in shape and are hinged at their outer edges to permit them to swing out from the body. These commodes were veneered, had brass animal feet and lion-mask mounts. Other commodes had four drawers on each side, a central cupboard and four short spade feet.

On various of his satinwood panels are decorative paintings featuring the work of artists such as Angelica Kauffman and Michael Angelo Pergolesi.

His three part dining table had fourteen tapered legs, often with spade feet and inlay on the legs. Banded inlay surrounds the table frame.

Among his tables were drop-leaves with one square and one oval end. Two such tables could be placed together to form a longer one.

Two years after Hepplewhite's death, in 1786, a catalogue called *The Cabinet-Maker and Upholster's Guide* was published. A second edition followed the next year and a third in 1794. This was the most serviceable catalogue to be issued in two decades—it had three hundred illustrations and was more technically accurate than Chippendale's earlier one.

Hepplewhite is associated with the Prince of Wales as the prince's chair-maker. Some historians dispute this association and say no evidence exists. However, a Hepplewhite design of a chair-back with a feathered motif within the shield is known as the "Prince of Wales plumes."

Thomas Sheraton, a Baptist preacher and drawing master, was another of the important late Georgian designers. He was influenced by the Adam brothers, Hepplewhite and Louis XVI furniture. Not only did Sheraton preach and write religious books, but his manuals of design, especially *The Cabinet-Maker and Upholster's Drawing Book* (1791), made Sheraton's mark in design history. He and George Hepplewhite were the major influences on America's Federal period. Sheraton is the link between Neo-Classical Adam and the Regency period that followed.

Sheraton designed his furniture to be made of mahogany and satinwood. However, American Sheraton pieces were often executed in mahogany with maple.

The urn was to Sheraton what the shell was to Queen Anne design.

The typical Sheraton chair combined fine lines with a square back and thin turned front legs, usually of carved mahogany. Various other chairs had japanning, were painted and had cane seats.

Sheraton used rectangular instead of curved shapes. His square-back chairs differed from the serpentine shape of Chippendale and the shield shapes of Hepplewhite. The backs were interlaced and rectangular, often with the central panel rising above the top-rail. Bannister backs and oval backs were favored as well. Round, reeded legs were his signature as were reeded columns and outcurved columns. Tambour shutters were effective on desks and bedroom pieces.

Sheraton continued the Adam and Hepplewhite sideboard design but added a brass "stay-rail" with the uprights often terminating in an urn finial.

Sheraton designed serpentine front game tables with reeded legs that had carved foliage on the upper part of the leg. He, like Hepplewhite, made a three part dining table; his with reeded legs and brass castors.

Another piece was his sofa table, in satinwood and rosewood, with splayed legs, drop-leaves, a long stretcher and round brasses.

Sheraton's later work reflected the demand for French Empire furniture. He created many "harlequin" pieces (disguised furniture) such as a library table concealing a step ladder or a dressing table that hid a washstand. He devised an ottoman with heating urns beneath to keep the seat warm in winter. This design anticipated the heated seats ultimately used on streetcars, buses and trains.

There are differences between Hepplewhite and Sheraton worth noting. Instead of the serpentine front of Hepplewhite's sideboard, Sheraton preferred a complete convex or a single swelling that was set between square ends. His upholstery differed from Hepplewhite's in that he revealed the seat frame instead of entirely concealing it.

REGENCY 1800-1830

The Regency period produced a body of furniture largely without dramatic shapes. Money was tight as a result of the French War and rising costs. Wood-working machines were being adapted to furniture manufacturing and the level of craftsmanship in general was falling. Marquetry was no longer in vogue, carving was required less often and the number of highly skilled carvers had begun to diminish.

Highly decorative veneers and ebonizing were popular. They were used with brass inlay, brass galleries, brass colonettes, brass bead moulding, wire lattice-work, cast metal feet and brass lion-mask mounts.

The principal woods used were mahogany and rosewood. Beechwood was used for painted furniture.

Strangely, an amateur named Thomas Hope inaugurated a new direction in design during the first decade of the Regency period. He was inspired by French influences combined with a love of Greek antiquity. Hope was a banker, a scholar, an amateur architect and a collector of antiques, who also designed furniture. His pieces took large geometric forms, some with caryatid supports, and he enlarged the klismos chair seen on Greek vase paintings.

The designs of Sheraton continued to influence furniture design of this period. The earlier decades of the nineteenth century were also influenced by contemporary French Empire styles. The Prince Regent who later became George IV had a liking for French eighteenth century furniture, and he commissioned pieces using cut-brass and tortoise-shell inlay. Thus, while this furniture was Regency in design, it also had a French flavor.

The influence of French furniture was also the result of the French Revolution, when many fine pieces were sold to English collectors by desperate French aristocrats.

George Bullock was an English designer who drew on existing Regency designs, interpreting them in massive size with gilt-bronze mounts and panels of cut-brass inlay in floral patterns. Marble tops suited these pieces.

About 1810, there was a vogue for Egyptian designs including lotus leaves, Egyptian heads and anthemion. Lion supports as well as these heads often formed the apex of pilasters.

Black and gold lacquered furniture in "Oriental taste" was popular as were caned chairs framed with imitation bamboo. Various chairs had a tub shaped back with upholstering on the seat. The arm rests were lion-mask and the feet were claw. The chair was ebonized, had gilt on the masks and feet, along with other chosen details.

The Chinese taste was revived and japanned furniture became ornate with pagodas, dragon designs and figures of Chinese men.

Many chairs assumed a Grecian mode with incurved legs. Sofa ends had unequal sizes and an arm rest was substituted for the solid back. "X"-frame stools and chairs made a return.

Long tables made in sections were popular. The sections were bolted together, and the supports were often central turned columns terminating with curved legs. Other dining tables were made with a pillar-and-claw base, usually four claws to a pillar. A circular table with a heavy circular base was also in use.

The sideboard table with carved lion monopodia (one foot) supports, a brass gallery and shallow drawers in the frieze, was a Regency piece. Another type of sideboard table had pedestal supports and cellarets. Late in the period, sideboards were enlarged, and became massive pieces.

An accessory dining room piece was the "super canterbury" designed to hold silverware. It was a deep partitioned tray with one semi-curved end and four turned legs.

After 1810, the columns on bow or straight-fronted chests of drawers were spirally reeded. Lion-masks and ring handles added to their design.

The bracket foot was replaced with a taller turned foot.

Regency style survived into the early years of the Victorian period.

VICTORIAN 1830-1900

The Victorian period in England emphasized self-expression. The population had grown from seven and a half million in 1780 to eighteen million in 1850. The desires of this population created a variety of styles. It was a romantic, sentimental and eclectic period that celebrated the home. This period marked the beginning of the emergence of women's rights with a greater participation by women in every aspect of English life.

Victorian furniture embraced previous world furniture designs and the English Victorians took many of these styles to their acquisitive hearts.

The furniture produced was not original or consistent in design, but for the burgeoning middle class in particular, it was "feel-good furniture." (I call it "soul furniture.") Prior to this time, only the rich and important people had fine furniture. Now in the mid-1800s people finally had the resources to acquire objects beyond the bare necessities. For the first time, there was enough furniture to go around.

Britain led the world in industrialization and was the most powerful nation in the nineteenth century. The middle class was a home-loving group and their homes reflected the new prosperity with solid furniture, carpets, heavy curtains and clutter. Collections for their cabinets and etageres were important.

The population expansion and wealth went hand in hand with the Industrial Revolution. The introduction of machinery and the improved ability to deliver were factors at variance with the conditions that had produced the old system of craftsmanship. Where previously the need was to furnish the best for a limited society, there was now a broad demand. This new group wanted an "instant background" with furniture that looked elegant to them and that would show their "good taste." The desires of the middle class had a tremendous effect on manufacturers, and their efforts to please created pieces that provide Victorian furniture with much of its fascination for our generation.

The Exhibition of 1851 provides us with an index of the wide variety that was popular in England at the time. The list includes Naturalism, Louis XIV, Elizabethan and Gothic styles. It highlighted the use of new materials, techniques and technical devices. The Victorians were fascinated with technical progress! New developments such as papier-mache received immediate publicity that delighted the manufacturers. Ornamental cast-iron was another widely used material for furniture, displaying a variety of design and great technical virtuosity. The marble industry which dated back to the eighteenth century now expanded. Prince Albert accepted the presidency of the Society of Arts and was a promoter of design, expressing an interest in carving. The majority of Victorian carving, however, has a mechanical quality, and by the end of the nineteenth century carving was no longer a popular decorative design element.

A distinctive feature of early Victorian furniture was the rounded form of most pieces, whatever their style. This is clearly seen on sofas, sideboards and the balloon back chair.

An interest developed in new materials and new ways to design furniture and the result was called "experimental furniture." Iron, wire, brass, papier-mache, marble and horn were used.

The Victorians recycled designs based on all periods. The styles included Tudor, Gothic, Elizabethan, French Louis XVI, Rococo, Italian Renaissance, Egyptian and Japanese. More than one influence could be found on a single piece, but the following characteristics were those principally associated with the major styles:

Gothic Revival featured pointed (lancet) arches and rounded arches, octagon shaped columns, tudor roses, trefoils and carving. For example, a Victorian Gothic armchair might have the back-rail curved in three arch forms, the center arch pointed, arch decoration under the arm-pads and trefoil designs enclosed in diamond shapes carved on the seat-rail.

Elizabethan designs included ball and spiral turnings, carved foliage and flowers. Chairs had high open backs filled with these designs. An example would be a chair with spiral-turned back stiles with finials, spiral-turned front legs and spiral-turned stretchers; the back legs were often plain. The back might also have an upholstered center with a carved crest-rail.

French Rococo Louis XV influences were seen in "C" and "S" naturalistic curves, scroll feet, cabriole legs and carving. Typical would be a dressing table with cabriole legs with foliate carving, and naturalistic carving around the mirror, with a curved shape. Many chairs were made with Rococo outlines.

The Louis XVI designs are characterized by angular lines, porcelain, ormolu, plaques, ebonized wood, inlay, urns and columns. An example would be a giltwood sofa with a straight back, narrow columns above the arms attached to the crest-rail, an upholstered buttoned back and seat. Padded arms and straight turned legs with castors completed the design.

Neo-Greek designs contained classical mouldings, columns, plinths and Greek key motifs.

Renaissance designs included masks, acanthus, scrolls, flowers, pediments, columns, cartouches, brackets and incised carving. Examples include a chair with a cartouche in the crest-rail or an ebony cabinet with ivory inlay in the Italian Renaissance style.

Jacobean influences show strapwork, intertwined designs and the use of oak. An example would be an oak double-sided desk, the sides displaying iron strapwork, with egg and dart moulding along the edges.

Oriental influences include bamboo turnings, lacquered cabinets, fret-work and panels. Examples of this influence are on many art (aesthetic) furniture pieces such as an ebonized cabinet with a centered Japanese panel in the center door and spindles.

No list of designs would be complete without mentioning papier-mache. Papier-mache pieces are delightful additions to contemporary homes, and collections can still be formed of this decorative furniture and articles like boxes, trays and frames.

"Papier-mache" was originally the French term for pulped paper although this process originated in the Orient. It is a technique which is associated primarily with the English Midlands. The English product in the 1820s was formed by paper laid in sheets and pasted together over a mold; it was then stoved to render it durable. (The process was said to be invented by Henry Clay in 1772.) During the Victorian period its production became an important trade because the pieces were suitable for japanning and polishing. Many pieces were inlaid with pearl and were also enriched with painted decorations. Papier-mache decoration was enhanced around 1825 by the introduction of mother-of-pearl, which was embedded into the varnish before it fully dried. Many tilt-top tables were made in this manner.

The original home of the papier-mache trade was Birmingham. Jennens and Betridge, and Charles Bielefeld extended the range of furniture made in this medium. Good quality pieces reached a peak about the middle of the century. Many wonderful pieces of papier-mache were made in these years such as lovely boxes, glorious pianos, exquisite chairs, beds, frames, tables and trays that now make fine tray tables. By 1865, however, papier-mache was no longer fashionable. Papier-mache pieces, however, are still available in antique shops and at antique shows.

Many collectors love English fantasy furniture. The Prince Regent, creator of the Brighton Pavilion is considered the world's first modern father of fantasy furniture. These pieces include a wide variety of chinoiserie examples. Other fantasy pieces include such off-beat creations as settees with dragon supports, cast-iron hall trees with antlers and bordello furniture.

Perhaps the most original furniture designed at this time were the bentwood pieces made by the Austrian, Michael Thonet. About 1830, Thonet developed a series of new processes for bending beechwood frames to a required shape with the use of steam and heat, and invented machines for a mass production line. Thonet also introduced the fantastic rocker. The first model had a leather buttoned seat and back plus great stability. Bentwood furniture was sold in great quantities in England throughout the last half of the nineteenth century.

Two other designers who must be mentioned are C.F.A. Voysey and C.R. Mackintosh, whose work had enormous influence. Charles Mackintosh is famous for his tall back chairs with motifs such as the weeping rose or wide vertical splats, often with an ovoid top-rail. Vosey, also a member of the Arts and Crafts Movement, was famous for his heart-shaped designs in furniture ornamentation. His style later became regarded as Art Nouveau.

The term "art furniture" or "aesthetic movement" was applied to pieces that were often ebonized, with painted or covered panels, bevelled-edge mirrors, brackets, spindles, shelves and Oriental influences. Anglo-Japanese motifs and shapes are seen from 1865 to 1890 with derivative mounts, fret glazing bars and Oriental shapes such as a modified pagoda cornice. Some of these pieces bring to mind a Gallic presence, especially the simpler sideboards with spindles as their primary decoration.

The Arts and Crafts movement, inspired by William Morris and William Ruskin, among others, sought the return to non-machine furniture. Rural handicrafts, as well as commercial pieces, were made with rush seats, oak wood, simple lines and the use of geometric inlay. In America, Gustav Stickley was responsible for the early twentieth century revival of furniture in the styles of the English Arts and Crafts movement.

Charles Eastlake was an influential English writer who wrote *Hints on Household Taste*, published in 1868. This was a widely published and influential book both in England and America. It discussed all elements in a home including dishes and lighting. Eastlake created interest in the "early English style," the main characteristics were use of medieval designs attached with pegged joints without the use of glue. He delighted in stain-glass panels and spindled galleries. Eastlake became identified with Gothic and Renaissance Revival furniture. Although he did actually make some furniture designs, "Eastlake furniture" was designed primarily by manufacturers who cashed in on his appeal and produced pieces far removed from his original design ideas. "Eastlake furniture" was sold in England and America. Charles Eastlake was not pleased, but apparently did nothing to stop his name from being used. It added to his importance and probably to his purse.

In the early twentieth century, there were many reproductions of previous historic styles, notably Jacobean, Queen Anne, Chippendale and Sheraton. The 1930s, influenced by the Victorian age, brought modernism with laminated wood, tubular steel, exotic woods and new shapes.

COLLECTING AND BUYING

Collecting and buying is what antique lovers do best. Our adventures keep the adrenaline flowing, and bad knees and aching feet are forgotten. Why? Because it is exciting to search for treasure, and we are all looking for that special piece.

Whether we are building a collection or furnishing our homes with English antique furniture, "the buy of a lifetime" is our goal. We may not get everything we desire, but let's give it a good try. *We are in a soft English furniture market.* Prime pieces, however, are always expensive, such as a pair of George II consoles that recently fetched $594,000. A soft market provides the best opportunities for the buyer and the collector. Now is the time!

With intelligent purchasing it is possible to acquire antique English furniture for what good new pieces cost. Antique furniture will always be an investment.

I am convinced that it is foolish to settle for reproductions when period pieces, or "in the style of" furniture from the nineteenth century are available. With antique pieces the buyer gets period design and tradition, warmth and charm. Besides, the purchaser can turn around and sell antique furniture the next day at an auction. Historic antique furniture is a solid investment for the present and will continue to provide pleasure for many future generations.

Old wills and inventories list household furniture and how the pieces were to be distributed. This is something worth considering.

All of us naturally gravitate to one particular period and style. Wandering through a showroom filled with equally fine pieces, your eyes will unerringly track a particular design period. You may admire, study or discuss buying, but in the end you will buy what is most appealing to you. This is the furniture you should build your collection around, because this is what you truly love.

Perception and current tastes change, but the furniture itself remains the same. Twenty-five years ago Victorian furniture was not generally appreciated. Today, some of these pieces are more expensive than earlier handmade ones. Victorian Gothic furniture was usually kept in the hall, but now these designs are in demand. If you buy what reflects your individual taste, you will ultimately reap a reward. I find that living with furniture I enjoy gives me pleasure every single day.

Contemporary homes with good contemporary furniture take on a new dimension and glow with the addition of a single Georgian armchair, a William and Mary burr veneer bureau or a Queen Anne tea table. Rooms do not have to be all one period. Objects belonging to different periods actually have a common denominator and live well together. Primitive art paired with Georgian Chippendale furniture coexist just fine, although we might intellectually reason that Tudor and Primitive are more fitting companions.

A collection doesn't need every example of existing period designs, and often can be more interestingly assembled with tight limits. An eclectic mix pleases some collectors.

You must be concerned about and prepared for the possibility of forgeries. I hope after reading the chapter on clues and chicanery you may have a better understanding of faking.

It is prudent to buy from established dealers who constantly handle English antique furniture and who in turn buy from reputable sources. Many dealers and their sales persons have become close friends of mine because we share a common interest. It is important to spend time with those on the same wave length.

Dealers will often allow you to try a piece of furniture in your home. They usually require payment in full, but will immediately destroy your check if the piece is returned. For the undecided, this is very helpful. Dimensions can be deceiving.

Auction houses are another source. Have you ever attended a "viewing" where the items to be auctioned can be inspected? The first time is actually intoxicating. Catalogues are very important because they will educate you as well as suggest price levels.

If you intend to bid, be sure you can identify the item. Pay attention to cracks, patina, mounts, warping or whatever catches your eye.

If you can't attend the actual auction, consider a "closed or pocket bid." I am a believer in leaving "absentee bids." You may be happily surprised when you are "the winner." If you do attend, *set a realistic price above which you will not go.* Remember, you will also pay a buyer's premium. It is a practical idea to subscribe to catalogues featuring antique English furniture. They are excellent reference material.

What about house sales? If you have a good eye and a working knowledge of antique furniture, bargains may exist. Maybe your name is on a Victorian love seat. Even if the furniture is disappointing, perhaps you will find a sterling cake server or an iron garden seat.

What about places like the Chicago Merchandise Mart? Facilities like this one are known to be "trade only," but many show rooms will allow you access if you carry a letter from a retail dealer to whom your purchase can be charged and delivered.

I caution you about making large furniture investments at antique shows. Are you familiar with the management? Have the dealers been vetted—able to expertly check and approve antiques? Is there an address where the dealer can be reached? At fine shows such as the Navy Pier Show in Chicago, I would not worry, but I frequent many antique shows that contain basically second-hand merchandise. It all comes down to how familiar you are with the articles you are hoping to acquire and how carefully you pursue your objectives.

Antique English furniture is also entering the office place. Georgian desks and partners' desks with fine leather wing chairs are an impressive sight. They are a deductible business expense, and when you retire they can come home with you. Check your local newspapers for antique show dates, auction dates and classified ads.

PRICE GUIDE

This guide consists of random examples of past and present antique English furniture auction prices. These prices include both English and American auction sales. The value of the pound versus the dollar is as follows:

1968 £ = $2.38
1969 £ = $2.39
1972 £ = $1.19
1980 £ = $2.40
1991 £ = $1.70

1961	**Four Regency chairs,** rosewood, gilded, brass mounts, circa 1810	$785.00
1991	One similar chair	$750.00
1961	**Georgian, Queen Anne design chair,** walnut, circa 1730	$350.00
1991	Similar chair	$1,500.00
1961	**Slant-front desk,** mahogany, fitted interior, bracket feet, circa 1770	$750.00
1991	Similar piece	$2,500.00
1961	**Eighteenth century corner cabinet,** mahogany, curved back, shaped shelves, fluted side pilasters, panelled doors	$875.00
1991	Similar piece	$3,500.00
1961	**Chippendale secretary bookcase,** mahogany	$700.00
1991	Similar piece	$10,000.00
1962	**Georgian tallboy,** mahogany, eight drawers, circa 1790	$685.00

Price Guide

1991	Similar piece	$3,000.00
1962	**Oak dresser,** top with three open shelves, middle section has two large drawers and three small, pot shelf in lower section	$785.00
1991	Similar piece	$3,500.00
1962	**Sideboard,** half-round shape, four legs with spade feet, circa 1770	$1,175.00
1991	Similar piece	$2,500.00
1962	**Chest of drawers,** walnut, panelled, teardrop brasses, bun feet	$675.00
1991	Similar piece	$2,500.00
1963	**Eighteenth century bow-front corner cabinet,** pine	$750.00
1964	Similar piece	$875.00
1991	Similar piece	$2,500.00
1963	**Georgian armchair,** mahogany, pierced splat, straight legs, circa 1780	$275.00
1991	Similar chair	$1,200.00
1963	**Hepplewhite washstand,** mahogany, circa 1790	$225.00
1991	Similar piece	$1,500.00
1963	**Regency armchair,** painted black with gold enrichments, circa 1810	$210.00
1991	Similar chair	$1,000.00
1963	**Spider-leg table,** mahogany, circa 1770	$425.00
1991	Similar piece	$1,500.00
1964	**Hepplewhite serving table,** mahogany, spade feet, circa 1790	$425.00
1991	Similar piece	$2,000.00
1964	**Sheraton sideboard,** mahogany, black inlay, pivoted bottle cabinets at each end, circa 1820	$875.00
1991	Similar piece	$3,500.00

1964	**Regency chair,** rosewood, ivory roundels, circa 1815	$225.00
1991	Similar chair	$1,200.00
1964	**Barber chair,** walnut, circa 1750	$150.00
1991	Similar chair	$1,700.00
1968	**Set of eight Regency chairs,** mahogany	£750
1985	Similar set	$3,500.00
1991	Similar set	$7,800.00
1969	**Gainsborough chair,** mid-eighteenth century	£100
1985	Similar chair	$1,700.00
1969	**George III upholstered chair,** leather	£100
1985	Similar chair	$7,000.00
1969	**Two pedestal dining table,** mahogany, circa 1800	£600
1990	**George III two pedestal table,** mahogany	$14,000.00
1985	**George IV three pedestal dining table,** mahogany,	$4,500.00
1990	**George II three pedestal table,** mahogany	$25,000.00
1969	**Victorian davenport bureau (desk),** walnut	£60
1991	Similar piece	$800.00
1969	**Pembroke table,** mahogany, circa 1790	£120
1972	Similar piece	£200
1985	Similar piece	$3,500.00
1969	**Chest,** mahogany, serpentine front, circa 1755	£500
1972	Similar piece	£750
1990	Similar piece	$12,000.00
1980	**Thonet armchair,** bentwood, circa 1860	£50
1991	Similar chair	$1,500.00
1980	**Canterbury,** papier-mache	£500
1991	Similar piece	$1,200.00

Price Guide

1980	**Victorian, Edwardian-type chair,** upholstered, circa 1890	£100
1991	Similar chair	$300.00
1980	**Oak chair-table**	£90
1991	Similar piece	$350.00
1980	**Mid-Victorian carved sideboard,** oak, circa 1850	£2,000
1990	Similar piece	$3,500.00
1980	**Jacobean chair,** oak, twist turnings, circa 1890	£70
1991	Similar chair	$100.00
1980	**Mid-Victorian open armchair,** mahogany, oval back, upholstered	£500
1991	Similar chair	$400.00
1985	**George III game table,** satinwood and mahogany, circa 1790	$2,875.00
1991	Similar piece	$3,500.00
1985	**George III card table,** mahogany and satinwood, cross-banded	$1,000.00
1991	Similar piece	$2,500.00
1985	**George I kneehole desk,** walnut	$4,000.00
1991	Similar piece	$5,000.00
1985	**Queen Anne tallboy,** walnut, bracket feet	$5,000.00
1991	Similar piece	$6,000.00
1985	**Queen Anne chest on stand,** walnut, circa 1710	$2,300.00
1991	Similar piece	$3,000.00
1985	**George III tallboy,** mahogany with satinwood panels	$1,200.00
1991	Similar piece	$2,500.00
1985	**Regency wardrobe,** mahogany, brass inlay	$1,700.00
1991	Similar piece	$2,250.00
1985	**George IV breakfast table,** rosewood	$1,600.00

1991	Similar piece	$2,000.00
1985	**George III pembroke table,** twin-flap, cross-banded with satinwood, boxwood lines	$3,000.00
1991	Similar piece	$3,500.00
1985	**Victorian ladies' writing desk,** inlaid walnut	$800.00
1991	Similar piece	$1,000.00
1985	**George II tripod table,** mahogany, with pie-crust edge and bird-cage support	$5,000.00
1991	Similar piece	$6,500.00
1985	**George III library table,** mahogany, circular, outcurved legs	$4,000.00
1991	Similar piece	$4,550.00
1985	**Mid-Georgian chest,** mahogany	$1,500.00
1991	Similar piece	$1,800.00
1985	**William and Mary chest,** walnut and marquetry, ball feet, circa 1700	$3,500.00
1991	Similar piece	$4,300.00
1985	**Early Victorian Wellington chest,** mahogany	$700.00
1991	Similar piece	$1,000.00
1985	**George III dumb waiter,** mahogany, three tiers	$1,300.00
1991	Similar piece	$1,800.00
1985	**Pair of George IV bow-front sidetables,** mahogany	$7,000.00
1991	Similar pieces	$8,100.00
1985	**George III partners desk,** mahogany, two pedestal, circa 1790	$5,000.00
1990	**George II style partners desk,** mahogany, two pedestals, mid-nineteenth century	$6,000.00
1985	**Late Georgian kneehole desk,** mahogany	$4,000.00

Price Guide

1991	Similar piece	$4,000.00
1985	**Set of George III dining chairs,** mahogany	$3,500.00
1990	Similar set	$6,000.00
1990	**George III chest-on-chest,** mahogany	$4,500.00
1990	**George I chest-on-chest,** walnut	$3,000.00
1985	**Regency circular table,** rosewood, scrolled feet	$1,800.00
1990	Similar piece	$7,500.00
1985	**George III sideboard,** mahogany, tapered legs, spade feet	$6,000.00
1990	Similar piece	$8,000.00
1985	**Kneehole desk,** walnut veneer, circa 1740	$675.00
1991	Similar piece	$3,000.00
1985	**George III tallboy,** mahogany, circa 1780	$1,600.00
1991	Similar piece	$2,500.00
1985	**George I stool,** walnut, upholstered, circa 1725	$1,550.00
1991	Similar piece	$1,800.00
1985	**Victorian center table,** walnut, circa 1880	$400.00
1991	Similar piece	$550.00
1985	**George III bureau,** mahogany, cylinder, circa 1800	$2,600.00
1991	Similar piece	$4,000.00
1985	**George II bureau,** mahogany, slant-front	$3,575.00
1991	Similar piece	$4,500.00
1985	**Six George III dining chairs,** mahogany, upholstered seats	$7,975.00
1991	Similar chairs	$9,000.00
1985	**Twelve Regency dining chairs,** mahogany, upholstered seats, circa 1815	$4,500.00
1991	Similar chairs	$7,200.00

1985	**Six George III dining chairs,** mahogany, upholstered seats	$7,975.00
1991	Similar chairs	$9,000.00
1985	**Six George III style dining chairs,** ladder-back	$850.00
1991	Similar chairs	$1,500.00
1985	**George III china cabinet,** mahogany, fret-work gallery	$3,575.00
1991	Similar piece	$4,000.00
1985	**Country Georgian style tea table,** straight legs	$350.00
1991	Similar piece	$500.00
1985	**George III pair of pedestals,** painted, carved, marble tops	$1,980.00
1991	Similar pieces	$2,500.00
1986	**William and Mary style chest on stand,** walnut, circa nineteenth century	$800.00
1991	Similar piece	$1,250.00

RECENT PRICES

1989	George II walnut secretary bookcase, second quarter eighteenth century	$8,500.00
1989	Two William and Mary carved walnut armchairs, late seventeenth century	$3,200.00
1989	George II oak coffer, second quarter eighteenth century	$1,300.00
1989	Six William and Mary walnut chairs, upholstered back and seat, baluster-turned legs	$4,600.00
1989	Jacobean oak chest, late seventeenth century, block feet	$650.00
1989	Mid-Victorian ormolu mounted, ebony side cabinet	$7,600.00

Year	Item	Price
1989	Regency parcel gilt and rosewood side cabinet	$19,600.00
1989	Late seventeenth century japanned and decorated cabinet on carved stand	$9,800.00
1989	Mid-Georgian walnut bureau desk	$6,900.00
1990	George III carved mahogany chair, pierced splats	$4,100.00
1990	Regency mahogany library chair converting to steps	$20,800.00
1990	Charles I oak armchair, panelled, mid-seventeenth century	$1,300.00
1990	Victorian carved walnut library chair, upholstered	$350.00
1990	Georgian mahogany breakfront secretaire bookcase	$20,800.00
1990	George III mahogany secretaire writing cabinet, with lattice fret	$15,300.00
1990	George III mahogany serpentine sideboard	$26,100.00
1990	Regency mahogany three pedestal dining table, with two leaves	$109,700.00
1990	E.W. Godwin occasional table, ebonized	$400.00
1991	George III late eighteenth century walnut tilt-top tea table	$500.00
1991	George III mahogany commode, third quarter nineteenth century	$700.00
1991	George III mahogany open armchair, last quarter eighteenth century	$800.00
1991	George III style mahogany linen press	$2,800.00
1991	Jacobean oak refectory table, first quarter eighteenth century, panelled top, baluster legs, rectangular stretcher	$4,000.00

1991	William IV mahogany bookcase, mid-nineteenth century	$11,000.00
1991	William and Mary oyster walnut chest, eighteenth century bun feet	$5,200.00
1991	George III giltwood armchair, pair, circa 1775	$2,300.00
1991	George III canterbury, mahogany	$1,100.00
1991	Pair George III style dining armchairs and eight side chairs	$8,150.00
1991	Four yew wood pub chairs	$800.00
1991	Four Windsor yew wood chairs	$1,000.00
1991	George III chair, pierced back, pagoda crest, japanned	$2,200.00
1991	George II corner chair, urn splats, mahogany, circa 1740	$2,640.00
1991	Regency library chair, opens to form steps, mahogany	$5,000.00
1991	Queen Anne chair, mahogany, slipper feet, solid splat	$3,850.00
1991	William and Mary chair, banister back, splint seat	$1,050.00
1991	George III serpentine front chest, mahogany	$3,580.00
1991	Chippendale chest, mahogany, three long and three short drawers	$2,450.00
1991	Georgian hanging corner cupboard, mahogany, circa 1820	$2,788.00
1991	George III bombé desk, four drawers, elm	$3,500.00
1991	George II lowboy, shaped apron, one drawer, walnut	$3,000.00

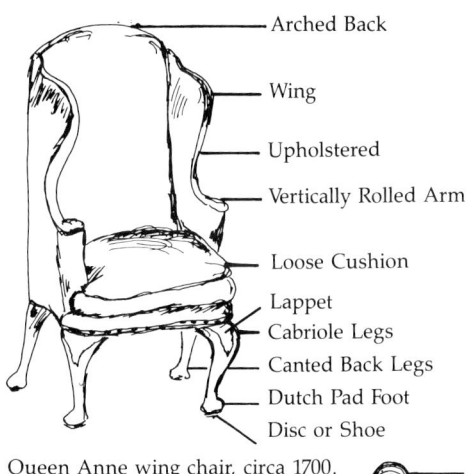

Queen Anne wing chair, circa 1700.

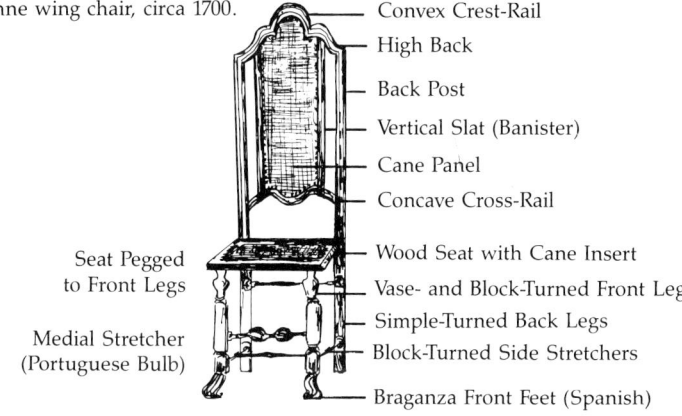

Cane chair, circa 1700 (painted beech).

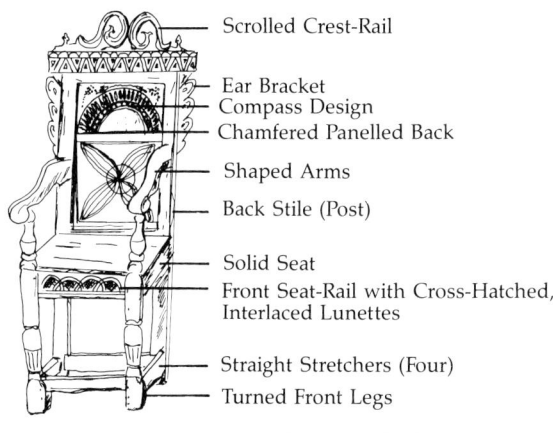

Panel chair, seventeenth century (oak).

Queen Anne cabinet on chest, burl walnut. The top section is beautifully fitted with drawers retaining their original brass drop handles and two small secret drawers are skillfully hidden inside. The cushion drawer in the frieze is faced with fantastically figured veneer. The base section contains two short over two long drawers with well-figured veneer and panel-effect herringbone inlay. The chased brass handles are old replacements as are the turned ball feet. Circa 1710.
Courtesy of Caledonian Incorporated, Winnetka, Illinois.

George I bureau, walnut. The top and fall, with four book matched panels of highly-figured veneers, are surrounded by herringbone inlay and cross-banding. The well-fitted interior includes pigeon holes and drawers faced with fluted columns. Two short over three long graduated drawers are all highly figured and inlaid. The brass handles are fine quality replacements. The bracket feet appear to be original. Circa 1720.
Courtesy of Caledonian Incorporated, Winnetka, Illinois.

George I chest-on-chest, walnut. The secretaire drawer has herringbone inlay and cross-banded edges. The combination of original brass fretted handles, seven original feet, moulded corners, and superb color make this piece an excellent example of early Georgian furniture. Circa 1720.
Courtesy of Caledonian Incorporated, Winnetka, Illinois.

George II bachelor's chest, mahogany, mid-eighteenth century. Courtesy of William Doyle Galleries, New York.

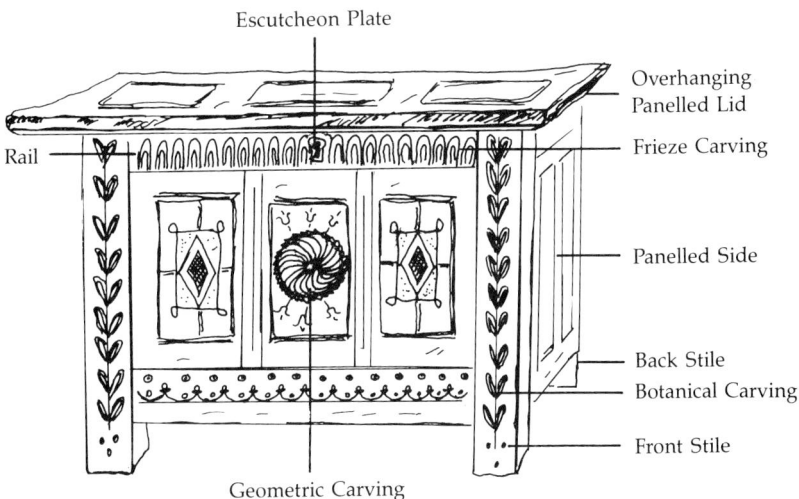

Chest, mid-seventeenth century (oak).

Early George II side table of graceful design and good faded color, mahogany. Cabriole leg, original brass handles and escutcheons. Circa 1740.
Courtesy of Caledonian Incorporated, Winnetka, Illinois.

George III tripod table with well-turned stem and slipper feet, mahogany. Circa 1750.
Courtesy of Caledonian Incorporated, Winnetka, Illinois.

George II drop-leaf table of smaller size, oak. Circa 1750.
Courtesy of Caledonian Incorporated, Winnetka, Illinois.

George III commode with boldly shaped three sided gallery, mahogany. Includes a removeable, shaped, sliding shelf over the lidded compartment with shaped apron. Circa 1760.
Courtesy of Caledonian Incorporated, Winnetka, Illinois.

George III bureau bookcase of classic design, mahogany. Note the top surmounted by an architectural moulded cornice with dentil moulding and a replacement gilt cartouche. The bookcase has typical thirteen pane glazing and adjustable shelves. The bureau has a fitted interior with drawers, pigeon holes and a leather lined writing surface. The base has four graduated long drawers with their original brass swan-neck handles. The ogee bracket feet are original. Circa 1770.
Courtesy of Caledonian Incorporated, Winnetka, Illinois.

George III breakfront bookcase featuring highly-figured, faded veneers and satinwood banding throughout, mahogany. The cornice has inlaid dentils and the frieze, inlaid lines. The drawers feature original cast brass handles. (Made originally as a wardrobe cabinet with blind doors.) Circa 1770.
Courtesy of Caledonian Incorporated, Winnetka, Illinois.

A large and important antique English fruitwood and elm chair with good pierced splat, shaped crest-rail and cabriole front legs. Circa 1780.
Courtesy of Caledonian Incorporated, Winnetka, Illinois.

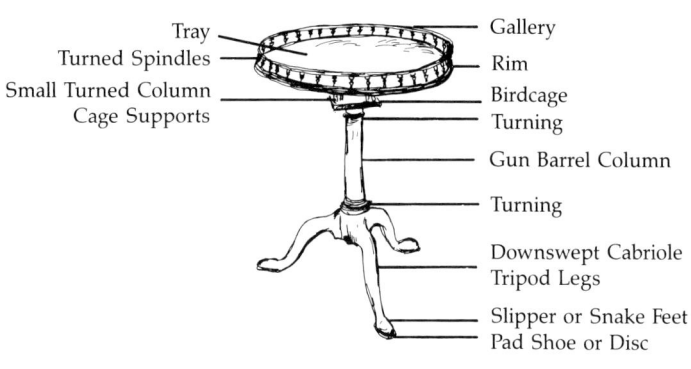

Tip-and-turn tea table from 1770 (mahogany).

George III Welsh dresser and rack, oak. The breakfront rack has an interesting center section with scalloped edge and "X" shaped fretted sides. The base has four long central drawers flanked each side by a short drawer and cupboard. The door includes central shell inlay. The fine brass swan-neck handles are original. Circa 1780.
Courtesy of Caledonian Incorporated, Winnetka, Illinois.

George III bookcase, mahogany, second half of the eighteenth century.
Courtesy of William Doyle Galleries, New York.

Pair of important antique English George III hall chairs, mahogany. Features a shaped back surrounded by foliate carving with central oval panel with carved ribbon motif, a dished and shaped seat over square tapering legs with fluting and block feet. Circa 1775.
Courtesy of Caledonian Incorporated, Winnetka, Illinois.

George III giltwood mirror, second half of the eighteenth century.
Courtesy of William Doyle Galleries, New York.

George III sideboard of fine quality and impressive size with outset shaped front, mahogany. Central drawer over arched frieze flasked by two cellarette drawers all with well-figured mahogany. The delicate turned legs are the best example of the period. Circa 1790.
Courtesy of Caledonian Incorporated, Winnetka, Illinois.

Provincial Georgian dining chairs each with a carved pierced splat back centering carved drapery, mahogany.
Courtesy of William Doyle Galleries, New York.

George III Sheraton Pembroke table of large size, mahogany. The top with rounded leaves is highly-figured and richly colored. The legs are delicately turned and there is a drawer in the apron. The brass handles and castors are fine quality replacements. Circa 1790.
Courtesy of Caledonian Incorporated, Winnetka, Illinois.

Pair of Sheraton satinwood arm chairs with painted decoration incorporating flower and peacock feathers and wrap over upholstered seats. Restoration to seat-rails. Circa 1790.
Courtesy of Caledonian Incorporated, Winnetka, Illinois.

Transitional kingwood small writing table. Includes a marble top and ormolu enrichments.
Courtesy of William Doyle Galleries, New York.

George III twin pedestal dining table, mahogany.
Courtesy of William Doyle Galleries, New York.

English George III architectural pine corner cabinet. Extensive blind fret-work and barrel back with marvelous 'shell.' Circa 1800.
Courtesy of Caledonian Incorporated, Winnetka, Illinois.

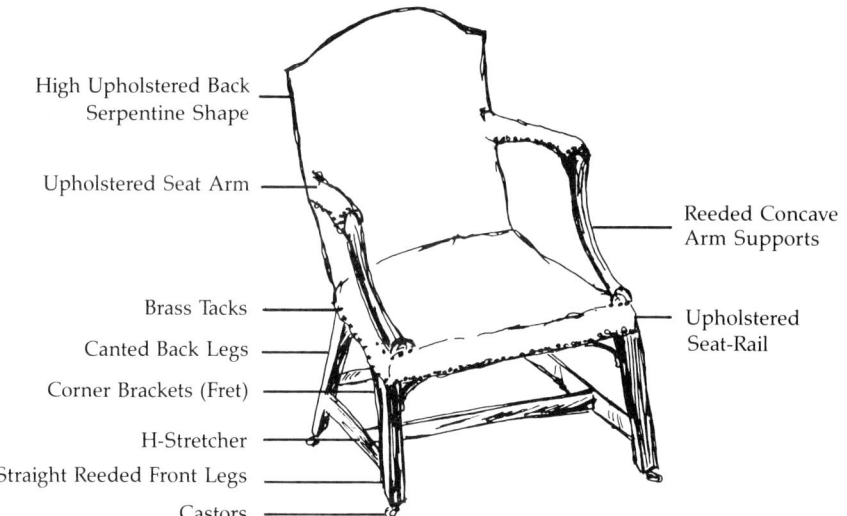

George III Gainsborough chair.

- High Upholstered Back Serpentine Shape
- Upholstered Seat Arm
- Brass Tacks
- Canted Back Legs
- Corner Brackets (Fret)
- H-Stretcher
- Straight Reeded Front Legs
- Castors
- Reeded Concave Arm Supports
- Upholstered Seat-Rail

George III circular pedestal breakfast or center table, mahogany. Unusual segmented top with cross-banded edge and apron. The base includes faceted stem and four downswept legs with ebony inlay. Good original cast brass caps with replacement castors.
Courtesy of Caledonian Incorporated, Winnetka, Illinois.

George III two-pillar dining table, mahogany. Note the tilting tops with reeded edges mounted on pillar bases with well-turned columns and four downswept reeded legs terminating in brass caps and castors. The two leaves, which are later replacements, extend the table to ninety-four and one-half inches. Circa 1810.
Courtesy of Caledonian Incorporated, Winnetka, Illinois.

George III bookcase cabinet, mahogany. Note the top section with bold moulded cornice over a pair of well-glazed, Gothic, arched doors. The base section includes two drawers over a pair of cabinet doors having interesting lozenge motif inlay. The lion-mask brass handles are fine quality replacements. Circa 1815.
Courtesy of Caledonian Incorporated, Winnetka, Illinois.

Provincial George III drum table, fruitwood, early nineteenth century.
Courtesy of William Doyle Galleries, New York.

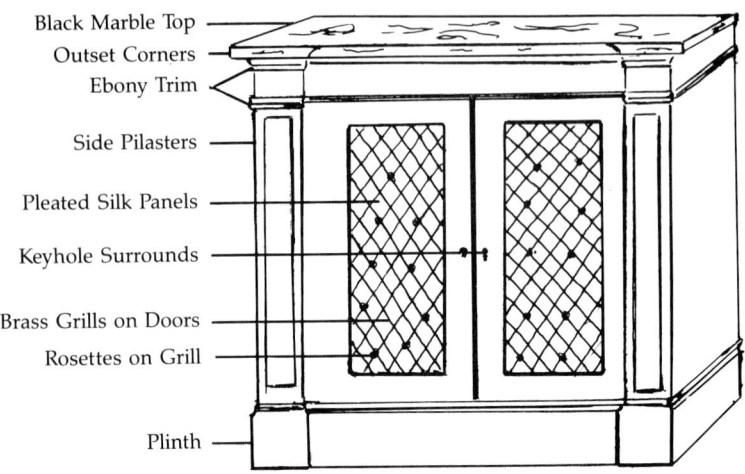

Regency cabinet, circa 1820 (mahogany).

Late Regency center table with well-figured tilting top, rosewood. Features tripod platform base with carved feet and castors and turned stem with leaf carving. Circa 1830.
Courtesy of Caledonian Incorporated, Winnetka, Illinois.

1991	George III secretary bookcase, mahogany, inlay	$5,650.00
1991	George III settee, giltwood, circa 1785	$5,550.00
1991	William and Mary settee, circa 1700	$3,900.00
1991	George III sideboard, bow-front, mahogany, circa 1790	$9,900.00
1991	George III table, side gate-leg, mahogany, circa 1800	$4,125.00
1991	Pembroke table, carved walnut, circa 1760	$6,600.00
1991	Regency serving table, mahogany, inlay	$8,250.00
1991	William and Mary style table, bun feet, oak	$500.00
1991	Papier-mache stand, circa 1850	$6,600.00
1991	George III window seat, carved, giltwood	$6,650.00

SELLING

While acquiring antiques we love is a pleasure, disposing of them can be a problem. The treasure now becomes a mere object. *Do not ignore the challenging adventure of selling.* (The value of stock investments are determined on the day they are sold.) Antiques give pleasurable dividends while you live with them, but also give a good return on investment when intelligently sold. The same can be said for antique English furniture.

You have choices when you decide to part with your possessions. *Do not settle for an inadequate price from a local shop just to get the piece or pieces out of the house.* Someone worked to get the best price when the piece was acquired. Don't be content with less than the best price when you sell.

You can't sell effectively if you do not know the market value of your antique. Look in shops carrying similar antiques, go to antique shows, check with an auction house or call in an appraiser. I have gone to homes to appraise one piece and said, "What about that one?" The reply was, "that old thing?" That particular old thing was an Arts and Crafts lamp with a singular shade worth a small lottery prize. At the very least look at a current price guide. Consider your options carefully. *Do not be lazy.* Selling wisely puts money *in your pocket* where it belongs.

Auctions are an option—a good option! Do you have an auction house nearby? Call their Consignment Department. They will put you in touch with an expert dealing with your type of item, or they will even send an expert out to your home if necessary. (I am heartbroken that many of our older citizens do not call a reputable auction house *before they give away furniture* and objects that would bring them money. Afterwards, they are sometimes very sorry that they did not know that their possessions were worth money. If they made only one hundred dollars on each piece, their nest egg would have increased.) Check with more than one auction house to see which one will do the most for you. *You can negotiate!* Ask questions. Ask what promotion they will give your piece or collection (request a photograph in the catalogue), and what services are available. Ask about packing, shipping and payment. Do you want a reserve? Will there be a seller's premium?

If you are not near an auction house, write to one or more. Describe your piece or collection, enclose a clear photograph and a copy of your original bill of sale if you have kept it. You will hear from them—auction houses are good about getting back to potential clients.

If you believe you have a rare piece or collection, I would suggest only major auction houses. Be sure your item will be in a sale of similar objects, insuring many bidders.

Another choice is to offer it back to the original place of purchase. Most antique dealers are delighted to recover an old piece they have already researched and profitably sold. You might make a deal for cash, or the dealer might take it on a consignment basis or take your piece in trade for a different piece. I hope you have saved the original invoice. *Any transaction should be in writing.*

Consignment means allowing a dealer to sell on your behalf for a percentage of the sale price. (You own the object until it is sold.) *If you put the piece on consignment, get the terms in writing.* The terms agreed upon should be on the shop's letterhead, dated and signed. Deal only with a person you trust to inform you of the price actually received. Only leave your piece at a shop that has a fast turnover. Otherwise, it could sit until you are nearly as old as the antique.

Donations can be a fast route if you need a tax write-off, so check with your accountant. In 1991, the government began allowing museum donations at "market value." Some charities will provide you with a receipt indicating value that will be acceptable to the Internal Revenue Service.

Classified ads are an alternative choice. Are you willing to allow strangers into your home? If not, a small piece might be shown at your bank where they have special private rooms.

Everything is worth something to someone.

Whatever arrangements you make, consider the physical welfare of the piece or collection. Whenever or however you dispose of your an-

tiques by sale or gift, be sure they remain in good condition and in good hands. Everything in life is lent to us and we, in turn, should see they will be available to future generations. That is the moral responsibility of the antique collector or inheritor.

VOCABULARY

Acanthus   A leaf design. The acanthus was a wild plant native to Southern Europe. Its beautiful ragged leaves were an important decorative detail on columns in the Classical period of Greece and Rome. The Renaissance revived this leaf design; the Queen Anne period carved them on chair knees; Chippendale carved them on front seat-rails and chair knees; Hepplewhite carved them on the ribs of shield-back chairs; and open, high relief acanthus scrolls are found carved on Victorian Rococo sofas and chairs. This design was important on other pieces such as silver.

Accent panel   A wood inlay of a contrasting wood usually in geometric shape.

Acorn   An ornament resembling an acorn. Examples are found adorning Tudor Jacobean chair back posts, and upside down drops on William and Mary highboy pieces.

Acorn finial   A finial taking its shape from an acorn. A finial is a decorative ornament that projects upward at the top of the furniture. Examples on chair back posts.

Adam   Robert (1728-1792) and James (1730-1794). English designers that created an English style after Chippendale. Noted for formal, Neo-Classical designs.

Aesthetic Movement (1865–1915)   Also called Art furniture or Art Aesthetic furniture. Term used in late 1860s and into the 1880s. Examples have ebonized wood with covered panels, bevelled edge mirrors, spindles, brass mounts, stamped leather and turned ringing. These pieces show Oriental and Gaelic influences.

Alabaster A granular variety of gypsum.

All original This means a piece that has all the parts it was born with, except for very small repairs.

Ambry A medieval cupboard, could be free-standing or built into an existing wall. Those with pierced doors were usually for food storage. Also used in churches for sacred vessels.

Amorini Winged cupids, gods of love or carved cherubs.

Angle chairs A corner or roundabout chair.

Anglo-Japanese (1865–1890) Also referred to as Art furniture and Art Aesthetic furniture. Often ebonized, might have stamped leather, turned ringing, brass mounts, spindles and bevelled edge mirrors.

Aniline Term applied to dyes derived from coal tar. Used to decorate fabrics after discovery in 1856. These dyes resulted in many rainbow hues.

Antefix An upright ornament.

Anthemion A Greek honeysuckle or camomile foliage.

Antimacassar A nineteenth century doily used, in the Victorian period, to protect chair backs from soiling because hair at that time was dressed with macassar oil.

Applied arm A separate, heavy, curved piece of wood at the back of certain Windsor chairs. Seen on "smoking chairs" in pubs. Also found upholstered on Victorian open-arm tub chairs.

Applied cresting A carved ornament attached to the top-rail of a chair or sofa. Examples on Chippendale chairs in the form of applied shells to their serpentine (cupid bow) crest-rail. Also on Victorian chairs and sofas.

Vocabulary

Applied decoration   A separate added piece. Examples are spindles and eggs glued on early chests, shell decorations added to embellish Queen Anne pieces, fret-work applied to Chinese Chippendale furniture and carved gadrooning applied to Chippendale pieces.

Applied molding   A molding, often geometric, applied to the face of furniture to create a panelled effect. Examples are seen on William and Mary pieces in the Stuart period.

Applique   This is an additional decoration, usually applied with glue. An example is the fret designs on Chinese Chippendale pieces. Can be referred to as applied decoration.

Appraisal   The worth of a piece, valued by an expert and usually done in writing. It is used for insurance, potential sale, or to settle an estate.

Apron piece   A skirt between the legs of the seat frame of a chair or between the legs of a casepiece. Casepieces with French feet have an apron piece. Examples are seen on Hepplewhite chests with French feet.

Arabesque   Decorative scrollwork or other rather intricate ornament composed of foliage, leaves and fruit, or of fantastic animals or figures.

Arcaded back   An arch back. A furniture back with an arcade design between the top-rail and the seat. Examples are seen on Gothic pieces, various Windsors and Sheraton chairs.

Arched aperture   An arched opening. Examples on George III corner cupboards with a stepped cornice above an arched aperture disclosing three shaped shelves.

Arched skirt   Also called an arched or arcaded apron. An apron designed with arcade shapes that may be round or pointed. Examples are seen on William and Mary mixing tables, highboys and lowboys.

Arched stretchers   Arched stretchers are arc or hoop shaped. Examples are seen on "C" and "S" scrolled stretchers of William and Mary chairs and on various Windsors. They are sometimes called crinoline stretchers on Windsor chairs.

Arches   Arches on furniture are usually round (Roman) or pointed (Gothic). Examples are seen carved on Georgian chairs.

Architectural furniture   Furniture in which the design includes architectural characteristics such as panelling. Usually in the form of large pieces. Examples of architectural pieces are wainscot chests and chairs, structural corner cupboards (perhaps with a shell carved dome) and fluted columns.

Arkwright   Medieval maker of chests (arks).

Arm pads   This is partial upholstery on the arms of chairs and sofas. Examples on Victorian sofas.

Arm stump   This is also called an arm support. It is the vertical piece which supports the front of a chair arm. Examples are seen on Victorian open armchairs.

Armoire   A press or wardrobe.

Art Nouveau (1875–1914)   This style is characterized by curvilinear motifs derived from natural forms, highly influenced by whip lash lines seen in Japanese prints. This design used Gothic and Japanese shapes. Henri Van de Velde and Emil Galle were outstanding designers of this style. The typical line is long and slightly curved, ending in a whip-like sharp curve. This style was most important in France. (English Art Nouveau is never as stylized as French and Belgian designs.)

Arts and Crafts Movement   Morris and Ruskin are associated with the movement that began about 1865 in England. Its ideal was the handmade craftsmanship of the Middle Ages. This movement clearly set a track for later designs.

Astrogel molding   A convex bead molding often used to overlap the joining of double doors.

Attenuated cabriole legs   This refers to slender cabriole legs.

Back stool   Form of stool with a back developed in the sixteenth century. Also an early name for an upholstered side chair.

Backsplash   A decorative backboard attached to a sideboard or washstand flanking the wall, ostensibly to protect it from splashed food or water. Some backsplashes have side elements like galleries.

Bail   A half-loop metal pull, usually brass, hanging down from a metal plate. Examples are seen on William and Mary, Queen Anne and Chippendale pieces.

Baize   A woolen fabric resembling felt, usually green, found on the tops of some game tables.

Ball-and-claw foot   A foot with a dragon or eagle claw holding a pearl or ball. This design originated in the Orient. Ball-and-claw feet appear in the early Georgian period, and are important on Queen Anne and Chippendale pieces both in England and America.

Ball finial   Brass or gilded wood ball decoration with a spear-like projection.

Ball foot   Also called an "onion foot." A boldly turned foot in the shape of a ball. Usually has a reel shape turning above the ball. Examples are seen on seventeenth century pieces.

Ball turnings   Turnings of closely spaced balls. Examples are seen on Elizabethan Revival pieces in the Victorian period.

Balloon back   A hoop-shaped chair back. Examples are seen on Queen Anne chair backs and Victorian upholstered chair backs.

Balloon seat A round, balloon shaped seat found on various Queen Anne, Sheraton and Victorian chairs.

Baluster A small, slender turning usually with a square base. These may be in a vase shape. Baluster turnings are an Elizabethan characteristic.

Bamboo The hollow, woody stem of the genera Bambusa. In the Victorian period, bamboo and rattan were often combined. Examples are dressing chests with a small drawer under the mirror and three drawers below.

Bamboo turnings Turnings simulating bamboo which was achieved by ringing. Examples in the Regency period.

Banding A band of colored inlay contrasting with the surrounding surface. Holly, maple, satinwood and ash were often used. Examples on Georgian Hepplewhite pieces.

Banister back Vertical banisters that are set or mortised into the crest and bottom rail of chairs. Examples are seen on William and Mary chairs in the Stuart period.

Banisters Also called "balusters." They are semi-circular spindles.

Baroque The Italian equivalent of French Rococo. Irregularly shaped and fantastic with conspicuous curves and broken scrolls. Chippendale was influenced by various Baroque designs.

Base The horizontal element on casepieces immediately above the feet or the bottom of a column.

Base molding Applied molding around the base of a casepiece.

Bat's wing brasses Brass handles and escutcheon plates that resemble a bat with outstretched wings. Some are chased, stamped or have punched designs. Seen in the seventeenth century. They were kept brightly polished to reflect firelight.

Batten A strip of wood used to cover joints between boards.

Bead and reel An ornamental turning resembling beads and reels strung alternately.

Bead molding Small semi-circular molding.

Bearer The rectangular section under a bureau fall which pulls out to support the fall when open.

Beau Brummell An eighteenth century dressing table named for the dandy of the same name.

Beech Used for painted Regency pieces. Michael Thonet used beechwood for his bentwood pieces from 1830 to 1900.

Bell flower A stylized flower with a narrow cup shaped with a flaring mouth and three to five clappers (petals). These stylized, usually hanging flowers or buds of three to five petals, are carved or inlaid one under the other, often dropping down vertically on the leg or on a chair splat.

Bell-seat A rounded, bell shaped seat. Examples on Georgian chairs.

Bench-carving A piece made separately and applied. The blazes on a Chippendale tall piece are an example.

Bench end The upright end of a church pew.

Bentwood furniture Designed by Michael Thonet from 1796 to 1871. Furniture was constructed from bent, solid lengths of beechwood. These pieces are original to the Victorian period. Thonet invented a process of moulding wood, after softening with steam, into structural shapes. Many types of furniture were designed with bentwood. Some chairs have cane seats and stamped decorations. Bentwood furniture, particularly the rocker, had a large English market.

Bergere A French word used to describe Louis XV style closed armchairs. A less common English word to describe this piece is a barjier.

Bevel A slanting, cutting away of an edge. Many Georgian bureaus (desks) have bevelled edges.

Bine The raised part of a spiral turning.

Biomorphic splat design Splat with shapes evoking images of biological organisms without representing any specific kind. It is usually used to describe splats having a Rococo style. Examples on eighteenth century Chippendale chairs.

Bird cage Four, small, vertical posts beneath the top of certain tip-and-turn tables. First seen in the early Georgian period on Queen Anne pieces.

Bird's-eye Small, brown markings resembling a bird's eye seen on maple timbers.

Blaze Another name for a flame or corkscrew finial. Examples are found on pediments or bonnets of casepieces on Chippendale pieces.

Blind doors Solid doors, often double, that conceal small drawers or compartments. The blind doors are between the glass enclosed top shelves, and the bottom portion consists of three drawers.

Block A square element, topping front legs, often with a centered concentric design. A mid-Georgian detail.

Block foot A foot shaped like a cube. When the foot tapers it is called a taper foot, therm or spade foot. In the Georgian period, block feet are seen on Chinese Chippendale straight legs. The spade foot on tapered legs is important on Hepplewhite pieces.

Block front pieces The center recedes in a flattened curve while the end curves outward in a flattened bulge. Not an English design.

Blocks Structural element used for bracing.

Board chest A chest constructed by nailing boards together to form a rectangular chest. Board chests are not as strong as panel chests. Nails, not dowels, were used on board chests.

Bobbin turning A turning resembling a wound bobbin. This turning is seen on certain Windsor chairs.

Bois durci Name given to imitation ebony carvings, of French manufacture, which were introduced in England during the Victorian period. Bois durci carvings were used to ornament ebonized cabinets and were in Grecian heads, rosettes and patera forms.

Bolection molding A raised molding having flat edges and a raised center.

Bombé An inflated or blown out shape. Bracket feet on these pieces often have a matching shape. Various English imitations of French commodes of the Louis XV period have the bombé shape.

Bookcase In England, bookcases, either fitted or contained in other furniture, were known from Medieval times. The domestic bookcase begins in the time of Charles II (1660-1685).

Bookend inlay Inlay resembling bookends. Seen on Hepplewhite pieces.

Bootjack legs   Legs of simple chests or casepieces that are formed continuations of the sides. Examples on early six-board chests.

Bordello furniture   Furniture related to sexual pleasure. Edward VII had his own specially created furniture for lovemaking. Pieces like a siege d'amour (love chair) were made in the Rococo style. This piece was designed to amuse him with two ladies at the same time.

Boss   A round or egg shaped ornament that was glued on.

Bottle turning   A turned detail of Dutch origin, so-called because of its resemblance to a bottle. Seen on William and Mary pieces.

Boucle   French word for curled. Indicates a curled nap on fabric.

Boulle, Charles   Celebrated designer of Louis XIV period. Noted for his inlay of metals and tortoise-shell work.

Boulle work   Type of marquetry using tortoise shell and metal. Perfected by Charles Boulle in eighteenth century France. Known as buhl work in nineteenth century English furniture making.

Boulton, Matthew   His Birmingham foundry produced metal ormolu mounts for furniture from 1762.

Bow-back   Eighteenth century Windsor type chair with the curved back meeting the chair seat.

Bow-top   A chair top-rail with one low, unbroken curve across its width.

Bowl turnings   Broader than a cup turning. Examples on William and Mary legs. Both are also called trumpet turnings.

Box settle Tudor and Elizabethan chest or box that functioned as a seat, often with a straight back.

Box stretcher Stretchers that form a rectangle.

Boxed ends A detail on particular Chippendale broken pediment tall pieces. They have architectural squared ends over the lower curve of the pediment, usually with a plinth and finial in the same design as the center finial (often urn and blaze). The box end is in line with the outer edge of the casepiece while the broken pediment extends slightly out in a concave curve.

Braced back This refers to Windsor chairs with two reinforcement spindles that project up from an extension behind the seat.

Bracelet Also called a collar, cuff or wrister. These are ornamental carved or applied pieces resembling bracelets, that appear on the ankles of certain cabriole legs, terminating in Spanish feet. Examples may be seen in the seventeenth century, often on dressing tables.

Bracket Reinforcement of the angle between parts or surfaces on a piece of furniture. A shaped bracket reinforces the joining of a leg to the seat-rail of a chair.

Bracket cornice A cornice moulding supported by brackets fixed to the frieze. This is a feature of Elizabethan and Jacobean furniture.

Bracket foot A foot supporting a casepiece that is attached directly to the underframing. A bracket foot can be plain, scrolled or molded. Bracket feet can be seen on Chippendale desks. A bracket foot on a bombé piece will outcurve to repeat the "kettle shape." These bracket feet are also called "swelled feet."

Brad Tiny nail that has little or no head, usually of brass. They are one inch or shorter. Used to attach applied moldings or brasses. Brads are seen holding William and Mary brass mounts in the Stuart period.

Braganza foot Named for Catherine of Braganza who became the queen of Charles II. Also called a Spanish foot. A curved-under foot, also called a Portuguese Flemish scroll foot. Found on turned, blocked and cabriole legs. Seen on seventeenth century furniture. (See Spanish foot.)

Brass-ball finial Ball finial with a spear-like projection.

Brass box foot A squared, brass foot, usually castored, often found on out-turned eighteenth century legs.

Brass furniture Term used by English merchants to describe furniture brasses and decorative furniture ornaments.

Brass inlay Designs like rosettes, stars, anthemion and thin strips; made of brass, set into furniture. Examples are found on Regency furniture.

Brass shoe A fitted, brass foot terminating in a button or castor.

Brass tacks Also called brass studs. Seen on William and Mary leather chairs, Cromwell chairs, late Chippendale chair seats and Hepplewhite chair seats. May be placed to resemble fret-work.

Breadboard ends These are wood strips matching the tabletop in width and thickness, and fastened to the top with wooden pins or hand forged nails. They protected the table ends from damage. Many country tables have this feature.

Breakfast table A small table with hinged side leaves. Originally intended for one person. They were first seen in Queen Anne designs. Pembroke and handkerchief tables are referred to as "breakfast tables."

Vocabulary

Breakfront   A cabinet having a central section, often a desk, extending forward from those, on either side. It usually has glass fronted doors in the upper section, and drawers or cabinets in the lower section.

Broken arch pediment   Pediment broken in arch shape. Also called a scroll top or swan-neck. Examples are seen on Chippendale tall pieces.

Broken pediment   A pediment (a pointed or curved piece used above the cornice on tall casepieces) with the moldings broken at the center for ornamental purposes. Seen on Queen Anne highboys. Greek and Roman temples were the origin for these pediments.

Brush foot   A Spanish foot that does not curve under. What we call brush feet may be damaged Spanish feet that no longer curve under.

Brushing slide   This is a large slide found at the top of many chests. Its purpose was to provide a surface on which the owner's clothes could be brushed.

Buffet   French word describing antique sideboards. It is also used to describe open doorless furniture of more than one tier.

Bulbous turning   A turned support in which a large bulb-like swelling is featured. Examples on Elizabethan and Jacobean pieces.

Bun foot   Foot, perhaps of Dutch origin, shaped like a flattened bun. A form of English bun foot is called a "melon foot." The English melon foot has vertical grooves while the American bun foot does not. Bun feet are seen on English William and Mary pieces in the seventeenth century.

Bureau   This piece began early in the seventeenth century as a small desk with a lifting lid made to stand on a table. In England, usually a desk, but in America, a chest of drawers or a dresser.

Bureau bookcase A Victorian piece. The top section was open or had closed shelves or a combination of the two. It also had a work surface that pulled out and a lower storage section. These pieces might have glass doors and painted panels or fret-work.

Bureau table A kneehole desk or kneehole chest of drawers. These are characterized by a single wide top drawer and tiers of narrow lower drawers flanking an opening that has a cupboard in back.

Burl veneer (burr) The growth, burl, from a tree trunk sliced for veneer. Antique veneer is thicker than new veneers. Used on late Stuart furniture. Many William and Mary chests featured burl (burr) veneers.

Butt-joint A joint formed by two pieces of wood united end to end without overlapping.

Button foot A round, turned foot. Examples on Sheraton tables.

Buttoning Upholstered buttons used to hold heavy upholstery in place. Examples in the Victorian period.

Buttons A turned, circular design detail found on the legs and stiles of certain Sheraton chairs. This detail was applied. Examples on some klismos type chairs about 1805.

"C" scroll A single convolute. Important in the seventeenth century; also a popular Rococo motif. Examples on William and Mary cane chairs, daybeds and upholstered arms of easy chairs. Also on various cabriole legs on the inside of the cabriole. Certain Rococo revival couches had "C" scroll legs. Mid-nineteenth "balloon-back" side chairs had pierced "C" scrolls on the horizontal splat.

Vocabulary

Cabochons Raised oval ornaments that were used as decorations. They were also called jewels. Seen in sixteenth century with strapwork designs and in the eighteenth century with acanthus leaves.

Cabriole leg Also called a "crooked leg." It is a leg that curves outward at the knee and inward towards the foot in an elongated "S" shape. This leg is Oriental in origin. The cabriole leg is first seen on late William and Mary pieces. It assumes more importance for Queen Anne and Chippendale pieces. Also important on Victorian Rococo pieces.

Caduceus Two serpents twining about a rod. Design seen in Regency period.

Cage work Any detail that resembles a cage. Examples on Chippendale tables.

Camel back A furniture back with a convex in the center, resembling a camel. Another descriptive name is "serpentine back." Chippendale designed sofas with this back.

Candle brackets Also called "candle slides." Small, sliding platforms built into a casepiece to hold a candlestick.

Candle drawers Narrow, vertical drawers. They are found on either side of the central locker in the interior of various slant-front desks. Also called document drawers.

Cane Made from stems of palms or grasses that were woven into a mesh. Originated in the Orient as a furniture material. Seventeenth century William and Mary chairs had caning; some Sheraton sofas were caned on the seat as well as the back; seen on various Regency pieces; and became important again in the Victorian period.

Canted Shape resulting when the corners of a square are cut off.

Canterbury A mid-eighteenth century, low, supper trolley. Also a mobile rack designed to hold magazines and music in the nineteenth century. Examples are seen in wood, bamboo and papier-mache.

Capital Projecting piece at the top of a column or pillar.

Capstan table A drum table (round), usually with drawers or shelves in the skirt, with a pedestal and outcurved legs.

Carcass The body of a casepiece. It does not include drawers or doors. It is like a turkey without wings, legs, head or tail.

Card table A folding table used for games. Also called a "gaming" or "game table." Some card or game tables have concave saucers, called counter-wells or guinea pockets, for chips. These tables might also have outsquared or outrounded corners for candles. Game tables, which continue to be made, were first seen during the Queen Anne period.

Carlton House table A writing table mounted on legs, which has a raised back and sides fitted with small drawers or pigeon holes. A late eighteenth century piece.

Carolean A term for pieces made in the reign of Charles I (1626-1649).

Carrying handles Usually of brass, these handles were on either side of a casepiece to facilitate moving the piece. Examples on heavy Georgian chests.

Cartouche An ornamental, scroll design or shield shape.

Cartouche-back A chair or sofa back shaped like a cartouche or scroll.

Carved tassels Wood tassels. Examples on Victorian pieces.

Caryatid A sculptural form of a human figure, usually female, used as the top member of a pedestal or as a leg support.

Cast-iron ball-and-claw feet Late nineteenth century design. Examples on dressing tables with an Elizabethan design.

Cast-iron furniture Made in England, on the Continent, and America in the Victorian period. A great amount was designed for gardens and summer houses.

Castor Small wheel on a swivel attached to furniture legs.

Cat's paw feet A foot resembling a cat's paw.

Cavetto cornice A concave shaped cornice. Examples on Queen Anne tallboys.

Cellaret A cabinet or stand for wine bottles.

Cellerette drawers End sections of sideboards, often curved, with several divisions; are often lead lined for storage of wine bottles.

Center table A table of various shapes that was placed in the middle of a hall. In the Victorian period, this was a popular piece and made in many designs such as Gothic, Rococo, Arts and Crafts, Chinese Chippendale and Sheraton styles.

Central locker This is the storage section in the center of the interior of a slant or slope front desk, with the document drawers on either side. Many lockers had secret hiding places behind them where gold coins were often hidden. Also called a prospect door.

Chair seats Chair seats are approximately sixteen to eighteen inches from the floor. Examples in wood, leather, cane and upholstery.

Chair-table A chair with a solid back that swings down on the arms to form a table.

Chaise-lounge A French word for a lounge with cabriole legs, with a molded, carved frame and a buttoned back.

Challis Also called challet; fine worsted wool.

Chamfered A shaped, bevelled edge usually at a forty-five degree angle.

Channel molding Grooved molding. Examples may be seen on Jacobean pieces.

Chasing A type of engraving. Early chasing was done with a pointed metal tool. Also seen on revival mounts in the Victorian period.

Chenille A velvety cord of silk or worsted.

Chequer Squares of contrasting color. Medieval inlay was often in a chequer design.

Chest Medieval box with a hinged lid. Drawers were added later in the seventeenth century.

Chest-on-a-frame Raised chest on a frame with legs under it. Examples are Jacobean and Queen Anne pieces.

Chest-on-chest Chest of drawers in two parts; a double chest.

Chesterfield An English term for a large sofa.

Cheval glass A mirror mounted so it can be tilted in a frame, usually full length.

Chevron borders A border consisting of strips meeting at an angle. Examples on Queen Anne side tables.

Vocabulary

Chiffonnier   A French word describing a work table of the eighteenth century with several tiers of shallow drawers. A high chest, or a bureau, or a low bookcase in the Regency period. In the late Victorian period, it was made as a dining room piece and called a chiffonnier-sideboard (1840s). Usually with a panelled door, a solid plinth base and a curvy back. Arts and Crafts term for particular dressers.

Chinese bracket feet   A squared, bracket foot with a curved inside with flat, squared pads. Examples in the Victorian period on cabinets circa 1889.

Chinese Chippendale   Chippendale style using Chinese or quasi-Chinese designs. Chinese Chippendale pieces are found on English Georgian pieces and in the American Chippendale period. Also in the Victorian period.

"Chinese taste"   Chinese designs such as a pagoda or fret-work. An eighteenth century term associated with Chippendale.

Chinoiserie   Eighteenth century style of decoration in which supposedly Chinese motifs were used. This form of decoration climaxed about 1750. Examples in the Georgian, Regency and Victorian periods.

Chintz   Originally any printed cotton fabric. Some chintz fabrics have a glazed surface.

Chip carving   A simple, low relief form of carving executed with flat chisels and gouges, usually in geometric patterns. This type of carving was done in the seventeenth century.

Chippendale   Thomas Chippendale (1718-1779) was an English designer in the Georgian period.

Classic period   Refers to ancient Greece and Rome.

Claw-and-ball foot A dragon or bird claw grasping a ball or pearl. Of Oriental origin. Used on Queen Anne and Chippendale legs.

Claw foot A paw foot. A foot made to resemble that of a lion or dog, or an eagle claw foot.

Claw table A small table with a circular shaped top, pedestal or shaft, and a tripod base with claw feet. Not to be confused with a pillar-and-claw table.

Clay, Henry Originator of papier-mache furniture about 1772.

Cloisonne The technique of covering an object's surface with vitrified enamels, separated by metal strips to create a design. Examples seen on table tops in the Near Eastern style late in the nineteenth century.

Closed arch An arch that is not broken.

Club chair A heavily upholstered chair having solid sides and a low back.

Club foot Also called a Dutch foot, this type of foot is found on a cabriole leg. Dutch or club feet may be in pad, ribbed, slipper and snake form. This type of foot may have a disc, shoe or cushion under it. Club feet are most important in the Georgian Queen Anne period. A second meaning is a tapering leg with a hoof shaped foot.

Cluster column legs These are leg columns placed together in a cluster. Examples may be seen on Georgian Chippendale and Sheraton pieces and on Victorian pieces.

Cock beading molding This is a tiny, half circle projecting molding.

Cockpen trellis back A geometric cage (pen) design that is found on George III chinoiserie chairs with a straight crest-rail and straight legs.

Coffer English term for chest. A medieval piece that became important again as a Victorian piece; carved, painted, panelled and inlaid. Some have heavy strap hinges of iron work.

Collar A round turning often found at the base of a ball or turnip foot, and on table shafts. Examples on seventeenth century pieces. Also a large turning, often carved, found at the top of various Victorian legs, sometimes with a smaller collar turning at the lower part of the leg.

Colonettes Small columns usually refers to "projecting colonettes" or "partial colonettes."

Combination chest This Victorian piece usually had a tiled splashback to the washstand section, a swing mirror and cupboard with a towel rack to the side. A combination washstand, dressing chest or table often with incised grooving across the drawers. The mirror side was often higher than the other side. Circa 1900.

Commode A low cabinet usually enclosing shelves or deep drawers. Can be called a bureau, console, chest or sideboard. This word usually describes chests of drawers, often associated with a French influence. Hepplewhite designed a commode in a demi-lune shape.

Commode chair Chair, with a deep apron, sheltering a chamber pot.

Compass decoration Circular, arc and star designs. Examples on Tudor chests.

Concave A hollow curve; a curve that dips inward.

Confidante An S-shaped sofa for two; one seat usually faced forward and the other seat backwards. A Victorian piece designed for whispering secrets.

Console table Table made in the form of a bracket with its back attached to the wall and its front supported by one or two legs.

Contrasting woods Important for early inlay, seen on Sheraton furniture (designed with mahogany and satinwood), and in the Victorian period.

Conversational Also called a confidante; a Victorian piece.

Convertible furniture An outgrowth of railroad furniture. Not to be confused with folding furniture which has a long military history. This was dual purpose furniture. The English called various pieces "harlequin" furniture.

Convex A rainbow shaped curve; a "camel-hump" shaped curve.

Convolute A scroll or paper-roll shape. Seen on various Chippendale crest-rails.

Corbel A bracket of slight extent. Examples on various Arts and Crafts pieces.

Corkscrew finial Also called a flame or blaze finial. Wood corkscrew finials are seen on Chippendale pieces.

Corner block A carved block of wood that was employed to strengthen chairs, set at the intersection of seat and legs.

Corner chair A square-seated chair with its seat placed diagonally so that one corner faces the front. A corner chair was called a roundabout or angle chair.

Corner cupboard Late seventeenth century cupboard, hanging or free standing. Type of cupboard which became fashionable in the eighteenth century. The front was diagonal or curved.

Cornice The horizontal molding at the top of a casepiece.

Cornucopia A horn of plenty. Motif popular on Rococo pieces.

Cotter-pin Wires that are clinched on the inside (twisted) of a drawer to hold the handles and plates of a drawer pull. They were easily untwisted to allow brasses to be removed for polishing. Examples in seventeenth century.

Couch Another name for daybed, rest bed or long chair.

Country Chippendale Mid-eighteenth century designs of Chippendale pieces made simply, often in pine or fruit woods by rural craftsmen.

Country furniture Furniture made in small rural communities of local woods, often primitive, but employing basic designs from the urban areas.

Court cupboard A sixteenth century cupboard popular until the Restoration. Had its upper portion enclosed and its lower portion open.

Court work Ornate English and European pieces made for the Crown and aristocracy. America made no similar pieces.

Crafts Movement About 1882, the Arts and Crafts movement preached a revival of craftsmanship.

Credenza Sideboard with doors often surmounted by drawers. Term to describe Victorian side cabinets.

Crescent stretcher Also called a crinoline stretcher. Has a semicircular shape. Examples on various Windsor chairs.

Crest-rail The top-rail of a furniture back. Crest-rails can be shaped, carved or both. William and Mary cane chairs had high-carved crest-rails. Victorian sofa crest-rails sometimes were covered with Rococo designed carving.

Cresting Ornamental feature added to the upper-most furniture part.

Cretonne Printed fabric of cotton or linen in all varieties of weaves and finishes.

Cricket table A rather small round table, with three triangular legs, often with a medial shelf. Jacobean examples.

Crinoline stretcher A semi-circular stretcher also called a crescent stretcher. Examples are seen on various Windsor chairs. They are attached to the front legs and supported by a short member from each back leg.

Crocket A medieval ornament which curves up and away from the supporting surface and returns partially upon itself in a knob-like termination. Examples on Gothic Revival wheel-back chairs designed in leaf and flower shapes.

Cross-banding A band or border where the figure of the wood runs across the width. Holly, maple and satinwood were often used for cross-banding.

Cross-hatching Shallow carving of vertical and horizontal lines imposed on each other. Examples on seventeenth century chests and chair backs.

Cross-rail A horizontal bar connecting uprights of a chair back.

Cross-stretcher "X" shaped stretcher found on occasional tables, various chairs, and on particular tallboys and lowboys. "X" stretchers are seen on many Rococo tables.

Cross-stretchered seating   Chairs, stools, sofas, settee bases and Roman curule chairs.

Crotch-grain   Veneer generally cut from the main crotch or fork of a tree.

Cuff   Inlaid bracelet on furniture legs.

Cup   Bottom or base of a turned shaft.

Cup-caster   A cup that fits over the end of a furniture leg with a pivot-mounted roller or wheel beneath.

Cup-turned   Cup shaped turning. Cup turnings are often used with trumpet turnings. Examples are seen on William and Mary tallboys.

Cupboard   Cabinet for food or clothing. In England, it was called an "ambry;" in France, an "armoire."

Cupid's bow   The top-rail of a chair back having a double ogee curve resembling a bow. It is called a serpentine top-rail. Seen on Chippendale chairs.

Curl   A natural figure in wood that resembles a curl.

Curule chair   A Neo-Classical chair resembling a Roman chair with curved half-circle legs in an "X" shape.

Curule legs   Half-circle legs in an "X" shape. These are also called Grecian cross legs.

Cushion drawer   A drawer set in the upper moulding or frieze of a secretaire or chest having a convex shape.

Cushioned pad foot   Dutch foot with a shoe or disk beneath the pad.

Cusp A Gothic detail consisting of a point or knob frequently carved, projecting from the intersection of two curves.

Cut down A piece with its legs having been shortened or "cut down."

Cylinder fall The curved, solid wood, sliding top fitted to writing tables or desks.

Cylinder foot A vertical, tapering foot found on Victorian Rococo cabriole legs replacing scroll or ball-and-claw feet.

Cylinder front A quarter round, fall-front of a desk that is either a solid piece or a tambour sliding up and back in quadrantal grooves.

Cyma curve (pronounced sī'mà) It is a continuous curve—half of which is concave and the other half convex. This produces a gentle "S" shape. An example is the cabriole leg.

"D" shape Refers to Georgian sideboards which have a "D" shaped top, and game tables with a "D" shaped top when closed.

Damask Named for the ancient city of Damascus where elaborate floral designs were woven of silk. It is flatter than brocade and reversible.

Davenport In England, a small writing table named after a Captain Davenport who commissioned it. Actually, the design was initially Georgian, and later a Regency piece before the Victorians took it up. The writing piece might have many small drawers that open on one side; the desk top slopes. In America, a large sofa, often one that converted into a bed.

Davenport table A narrow table with drawers having drop-leaves at both ends, usually placed behind a sofa or davenport. Also called a sofa table.

Daventry A small chest of drawers with a slant top. The story is that it was named for a client of Gillow's who claimed to have designed it.

Daybed A long chair, chaise or lounge that was used for day rest. The French term is chaise-lounge. Daybeds are also called "couches" or "rest beds."

Deal Scottish pine, pine conifer or wild pine used for interior parts of English casepieces. Deal was also used in England for cheap furniture in the Victorian period.

Decks Small drawers frequently placed on either side of Victorian chest tops.

Demi-arm A partial arm seen on Victorian seating pieces. It is also called a "hip rest."

Demi-lune A half-round shape. Examples on commodes.

Dentil molding Molding that resembles teeth that need braces because they have space between them.

Desk A bureau; a writing surface with or without drawers or cabinets; can be open or closed. Early examples in oak, in Tudor and Stuart periods. Evolved from a box on a stand. Examples were made in Elizabethan, Gothic, Georgian and Regency styles, to name a few.

Desk and bookcase form A bookcase having a hinged door opening to shelves or partitions added to a desk unit; also called a secretary.

Diaper Design consisting of diamond shapes in regular repeats. Examples on medieval chests.

Directoire Type of French furnishings and decoration of the mid-1790s, characterized by an increasing use of Greco-Roman forms and motifs. This is referred to as a Neo-Classical style.

Disc foot   Also called a "disk foot." A Dutch pad foot with a round shoe (disc) beneath it. Also called a cushioned foot.

Dish-top   A rounded table top that is dished out flat in the center leaving a rounded, raised edge. Dish-tops may be seen on dumbwaiters.

Divan   An upholstered couch without arms or back, originating with the Turkish custom of heaping piles of rugs together for reclining.

Divan-a-Turkish   Turkish inspired seat without arms or a back. A divan easy chair is the nineteenth century name for an armchair with a long seat and rolled-over arms.

Document drawer   Also called a "document box." A narrow, vertical drawer that is open at the top and is placed next to the central locker in a desk interior. Document drawers are found on English desks and secretaries.

Dog ear   A projecting, rectangular ornament. A Georgian detail.

Dog tooth   Early English detail consisting of a repeated triangular design.

Dolphin   A marine mammal stylized for furniture design. This motif appears on English, French and American furniture.

Doric column   Greek or Roman columns. The Greek ones do not have a base while Roman ones do. They are channeled and have a capital at the top.

Double chairs   Also known as "love seats." The English call them "Darby and Joan seats," and the French term is "confidantes."

Double feet   A double round or double block turning. Examples may be seen on seventeenth century cane chairs and bannister back chairs.

Dovetail   Devices used to fasten wood together by fitting wedge shaped or dovetail shaped pieces into corresponding negative spaces. Dovetails exist on ancient Egyptian furniture, proving that "if it works, don't change it." Examples of dovetails can be seen on Chippendale casepieces. Early ones are not uniform. A lapped dovetail conceals the actual construction and are found only on very expensive pieces.

Dowel   Headless wood or iron pin employed for joining two pieces of wood. Dowels are used in place of screws or nails. Also called a trenail (tree-nail).

Dragons's claw foot   A claw-and-ball foot. An eighteenth century foot with a dragon's claw grasping a ball or pearl. These are seen on cabriole legs late on Queen Anne designs as well as on Chippendale designs. The dragon's claw foot is Oriental in origin.

Drake foot   A Dutch or club foot carved with three toes, sometimes four, that somewhat resemble the contracted claw of a male duck. They are also called ribbed and trifid. Found on cabriole legs. They either could be stockinged or have a bracelet.

Draped torsos   Carved, draped, male figures designed to act as supports.

Draw-bore process   A fifteenth century device where the pin hole through the tenon was made slightly out of line with those in the mortice walls, so that when the dowel pin was driven home, it drew the tenon more tightly.

Draw-runner   A device for supporting the drop-lid or fall-front of a desk or secretary. These are also called slides.

Draw table Dining table which is fitted with leaves—one to pull out at each end. Examples in Elizabethan period.

Drawer blades The wooden strips that separate a drawer into separate sections.

Drawer bottom Lower portion of a drawer. (Note the thickness of drawer bottoms to identify origin.) English cabinetmakers used thin deal or oak, while American cabinetmakers used thicker boards of poplar, pine and chestnut. The bottoms of old pieces are not smooth like later machine-finished drawer bottoms.

Dressing case Victorian term for a dresser with a high mirror attached to a marble topped dresser, and usually two wide drawers at the bottom and four higher small drawers above. The center of the dresser part is lower at the middle. Many of these pieces were made in Greek Revival and Eastlake styles.

Dressing table Seen from the seventeenth century. Eighteenth century dressing tables for men were important.

Drop A pendant ornament. Examples are found on William and Mary tallboys and on Victorian pieces.

Drop-front Also called a fall-front. The leaf falls forward and becomes the writing place; it rests on draw-runners or slides.

Drop handle A pendant mount (hardware) used as a drawer pull. Important on seventeenth century pieces and later on Victorian pieces.

Drop-leaf A table with one or two hinged leaves which can be raised or dropped by bringing swinging legs or supports into position.

Drop ornament This is an ornament that hangs down, usually from the underframe of a piece. Also called pendants.

Vocabulary

Dropped seat A seat made concave so that its middle and front are lower than its sides.

Drum table Also called a capstan table. A round table usually with drawers or shelves in the skirt, a pedestal and out-curved legs.

Dry rot When wood shows frailty, cracking or breaking, producing a gray dry powder. Restoration is a necessity!

Dumbwaiter An eighteenth century piece which stood near the dining table. It was a tiered stand made to hold serving items. A portable sideboard usually with tiers of circular shelves, fixed to an upright axis. The shelves are larger at the bottom and castored.

Dust-boards Large pieces of wood placed between the drawers in English casepieces to prevent stealing. American casepieces do not usually have dust-boards, however, some appear on early Williamsburg and Charleston casepieces. Also on the work of a Boston cabinetmaker.

Dutch foot A club foot found on cabriole legs. If a shoe or disc (disk) is beneath it, it is called a disc or disk foot. Varieties include a pad, ribbed, snake or slipper foot.

Dwarf bookcase A small case made after the mid-1800s, often square, table height and may revolve.

Eagle heads Curved, "C" scroll carved eagle heads. If on a center leg, this leg has two reversed heads, one on each side of the leg at the upper most portion. Examples found on George II settees.

Ear-pieces The pieces glued at two sides of the top of a cabriole leg. They avoid an abrupt termination at the top of the leg. The ear-piece is also called a shoulder-piece in English furniture books. Another definition is an extension of a chair's crest-rail beyond the back posts.

Ears An extension of a chair's crest-rail or comb-piece beyond the back posts. When they are carved in a spiral they are called voluted. Examples are seen on Chippendale chairs with cupid's bow or serpentine back-rails. Also on various Windsor chairs.

Eastlake, Charles (1836-1906) An influential English writer. He wrote *Hints on Household Taste,* published in 1868. He created interest in the "early English style," the main characteristics being joined medieval designs, attached with pegged joints without glue. He delighted in stained-glass panels and spindled galleries. He became identified with Gothic and Renaissance Revival furniture. Manufacturers cashed in on his appeal and produced pieces far removed from his design ideas. They called this furniture Eastlake style in England and America. Eastlake was not pleased, but apparently did nothing to stop his name from being used.

Easy chair An upholstered chair which was first made in the seventeenth century. These were the first really comfortable chairs. Use of slip covers appear with upholstered furniture.

Ebonized wood Wood stained to look like real ebony. Ash and holly were frequently used for this purpose. Important for inlay. Entire pieces were ebonized in the Regency and Victorian periods.

Ebonizing Close-grained woods, such as beech or birch, which were stained and polished to resemble real ebony. Examples on Regency and Victorian aesthetic pieces.

Ebony and gilt drops Term (from a circa 1800 catalogue) to describe Victorian pulls. Pear shaped, black pendant mounts attached to a round, brass plate. Also called a teardrop mount after the early seventeenth century William and Mary teardrops.

Vocabulary

Eclecticism Adapting at will the forms of any previous period. The Victorian period is certainly eclectic.

Edwardian Pertaining to the reign of Edward VII from 1901 to 1910. Son of Queen Victoria. An example of a typical Edwardian chest of drawers would have a solid plinth base.

Egg and dart A convex molding with a design resembling alternating eggs and darts. Examples on eighteenth century Georgian pieces.

Eglomise' Named for a French eighteenth century artist. It is decorated glass in which the back is painted or gilded. Examples of eglomise' are found on Queen Anne mirrors.

Egyptian Revival (1865-1935) Napoleon's 1798 campaign in Egypt, and the discovery (seventy years later) of the Rosetta Stone, triggered interest in Egyptian designs. Most inventive pieces were by Thomas Hope. Examples are chairs with crouching priests supporting their elbows, winged Isis on the chair-rail and ornaments from monuments at Thebes. Other Egyptian designs were winged sphinx heads, winged orbs, palmettos, lion-paw feet, lotus, ebonized wood, and gilt and bronze decorations.

Egyptian taste A brief attempt to employ Egyptian designs around the turn of the eighteenth and early nineteenth century. Napoleon's African campaign, in 1798, brought them to France. English designers used them to some degree.

Elliptic front A round front. Examples on Rococo etageres.

Elliptical foot A William and Mary circular, turned foot found on various slat-back chairs with turned legs.

Embossing Fabric pressed between engraved rollers with heat to give raised effect.

Endive marquetry Also called "seaweed" marquetry. A pattern resembling flowing arabesque lines. Seen on seventeenth century tables and chests.

Endive scroll A carved ornament from the Chippendale period derived from the endive leaf.

English morning room A sitting room where the family gathered. Here they would play cards, sew and visit. A morning room piece might include a game table, a piano and a work table.

Escallop Also called scallop or shell. A flat shell with curved scallops.

Escritoire French word. A writing desk containing drawer compartments and pigeon holes, with one or more secret ones. The English term secretary (secret) was derived from this word. May also signify a simple writing table.

Escutcheon A shield-shaped piece that covers the keyhole. Can be metal, ivory or wood.

Etagere A series of open shelves. Many examples appear in the Victorian period. Some were made to stand in corners. "Whatnot" is the American description.

Extension table A table which opens from the center and moves in both directions in order to make room for loose leaves in the open part. Contemporary tables are often constructed this way.

Fake A copy of an authentic piece made to be sold as if it were "the real thing," or a piece composed of antique fragments that were not originally together. A fake is a piece made with intent to deceive.

Fall-front Also called a drop-front or slope-front.

Vocabulary

Fan Carved shell motif came to England probably from a Dutch cockleshell design. This stylized shell, with fluted rays in a half-circle (half-round), has many names. It has been called a shell, a fan, a rising sun and a sunrise, but in England, it is often called a sunburst. The most important design element on Queen Anne furniture.

Fantasy furniture A mix of Neo-Classical designs, nymphs, carved draperies, Chinese mythological creatures, cupids, dragons, blackamoors, mermaids, dolphins, shell chairs, flower chairs, leaf chairs and the like. This is great furniture and meant to charm.

Farthingale chair Seventeenth century chair with a broad seat and low back. Originally a woman's chair, it was later enlarged, given a foot stool and became a man's chair.

Fateuil A French word used to describe Louis XV style open armchairs.

Faun A legendary demi-god, half goat, half man. Used decoratively in the work of Robert Adam.

Feather banding A border, usually in veneer or marquetry, with two narrow strips laid at opposing angles. Also called herringbone banding.

Felt Wool, mohair or mixed fibers pressed into a compact sheet without weaving.

Festoons Strings or chains carved, inlaid, or painted to resemble ribbons, draperies, foliage or flowers.

Fiddle-back A single splat of a chair which has a fiddle shape. Narrow fiddle shapes are also called "spoon shaped."

Fiddle-string or stick-back Terms referring to the backs of chairs with the spindles resembling sticks or fiddle strings.

Fielded panels   Raised panels.

Figures   Timber designs, brought out by cutting the wood so that veneers or solid surfaces display various types of irregularities in the grain and in color. (Fiddle-back figures are found primarily in Honduras mahogany.)

Finger-grip   A groove indented in the lower edge of a drawer-front or on a wooden handle. These can be seen in the Victorian period.

Finger-roll   Continuous concave molding in the frame of a piece. Examples can be seen on Victorian sofa frames and chair frames.

Finial   A decorative ornament that points upward. Examples of acorn, knob and double knob designs can be seen on Stuart chairs, and on Chippendale casepieces such as tallboys and secretaries as blazes and eagles.

Fittings   The metal handles or escutcheons on furniture. Also called mounts.

Flame   A finial carved in a spiral or flame shape. These finials are also called a blaze or corkscrew.

Flat carving   Also called peasant carving, relief carving or incised carving. Flat carving is seen on Tudor chests.

Flemish curve   An "S" scroll. Examples on seventeenth century cane chairs.

Flip-top table   A card or game table with a hinged top, made in two parts.

Flower head supports   A Regency detail where the arm supports are shaped like an open flower into which the arm is attached.

Flutes   An inlay design resembling the musical instrument. Sometimes the central flute dips below the two side ones.

Fluting   A series of rounded, convex furrows or channels cut vertically on a column, leg, shaft, pilaster or canted edge. The opposite of "reeding" which is raised.

Fly rail   The swinging bracket which supports a flap or drop-leaf.

Folding cribs   Popular throughout the last quarter of the nineteenth century. Usually had castors and could be folded and pushed under a larger bed.

Foil   The point formed by the intersection of two circular arcs. A Gothic detail.

Frame   The basic skeleton of a piece of furniture.

Free-standing column   A column with open space behind it. Examples on Georgian Sheraton sofas.

French foot   A slightly out-turned, rather tall, bracket foot that is usually combined with an apron or skirt. Often seen on Hepplewhite pieces.

French polish   A solution of shellac dissolved in spirit and applied to a wood surface. Introduced into England from France about 1820. Several coats were applied, until a hard, glossy film covered the surface. May cause the surface of a piece to become cloudy or produce reddish streaks.

French whorl foot   A foot which is swirled or curled inward. Seen on various Chippendale pieces and also on Victorian furniture having a French Rococo flavor.

Fret-work   Ornamental work consisting of three dimensional designs that are within a band or border. They are an applied decoration.

Frieze A decorative band. Examples on English tall chests, at the top under the cornice.

Fringe Ornamental edging used in upholstering; made of twisted threads, yarns, tassels, etc. Made of silk or other materials, often with metal.

Fruitwood Used mainly for country furniture (apple, pear, cherry).

Gadroon edges A decoration resembling almond shaped reeding or fluting. Popular in late seventeenth century and second half of eighteenth century.

Gainsborough chair A high back, upholstered chair with open arms. Named for Thomas Gainsborough who painted many of his subjects in them. In America, the same style chair was named for Martha Washington (the Martha Washington chair).

Gallery An ornamental rail or cresting in wood or metal surrounding the top of a table, desk or stand. Examples in the Regency period.

Gallon Narrow binding of cotton, wool or silk, usually showing fancy weaves.

Games tables Also called card tables.

Garland A carved or inlaid floral swag.

Garters Seen carved, applied and inlaid on cabriole legs below the knee.

Gate-leg table Also called a flap-table. A table with fall-leaves supported by folding legs that resemble a gate. A late Stuart table, but still popular today.

Georgian English period from the accession of George I in 1714 to the death of George IV in 1830.

Gesso A plaster and glue preparation for under painting or gilding. On japanned pieces, gesso was thickly applied under the ground color to give dimension to the chinoiserie designs.

Gilded ball finial Round, onion shaped piece, gilded, with a spear-like projection.

Gilding A thin layer of gold applied to furniture. Entire gilded pieces are associated with English and French furniture. Gilding and japanning are seen on various William and Mary pieces and on Queen Anne pieces. Chippendale sometimes gilded shells and columns on his more highly decorated furniture. Robert Adams also designed gilded furniture.

Gimp Narrow tape of silk or cotton used for applique and for hiding tacks on upholstered furniture.

Glastonbury chair An "X" framed Gothic seat with a sloping panelled seat and a drooping curve in the arms. Originally an ecclesiastical chair.

Glazed Fitted or set with glass. Examples found on secretaries and bookcases.

Glazing bars Wood strips which frame the glass panes. Also known as muntins.

Gothic The Gothic period, 1150 to 1500, featured pointed lancet arches.

Gothic Revival period Victorian Gothic Revival was the early nineteenth century in England and America. It was more important in the English Victorian period than in the

American period. Gothic Revival furniture is becoming sought after at the present time.

Gouge carving   A type of carving with the designs gouged out with chisels. Examples of gouge carving are seen on early frame chests.

Grain painting   Technique of applying paint to imitate the grain of wood. Grain painting has a long English history.

Great chairs   Carved Tudor and Stuart wainscot chairs reserved for important persons.

Grecian cross-legs   Another name for curule legs. These are seen on Sheraton and Regency pieces.

Greek fret   Greek key pattern: repeated square, hook shaped forms. Often used as a band decoration.

Griffin   A chimerical beast usually having the head and wings of an eagle and the body of a lion. Used as a decorative motif.

Grooving   Incised carving. Examples on Victorian chairs.

Grotesque   Describes fantasy in the shaping of forms carved on furniture. Examples on early chests.

Guilloche   A sixteenth, seventeenth and eighteenth century design of braided, twisted or interlaced bands that form interlaced circles.

Gun-barrel turnings   A circular turning that narrows like a canon, usually combined with ring turnings. Examples on table shafts.

"H" stretcher   A stretcher in a "H" shape.

Hair cloth   A fabric composed of cotton warps and filling threads of horse hair. Black and very durable.

Half-column A split column set against a flat surface. These may also be called a rounded pilaster.

Hall tree A stand or framework of wood or metal used for coats and hats. They were made in many styles in the Victorian period. They often had a tray base for umbrellas or boots. Some were designed to hang on the wall, and often had a center mirror.

Handhold The end of a chair arm where the hand rests.

Handkerchief table Tables with a closed triangular top that forms a square "handkerchief" when open.

Handles See mounts.

Harlequin furniture A Georgian term used to describe disguised pieces such as a library table concealing a step ladder.

Hepplewhite, George (1785-1800) An English designer in the Georgian period who is famous for his shield-back chairs and graceful lines. A major American period, which immediately followed the Revolutionary War, is named for him.

Herringbone Inlay done with slanting pieces of wood.

Herringbone banding See feathered banding.

Highboy A chest of drawers that is on a frame or on a lowboy. The lower part has one long drawer or two smaller ones. The word "highboy" is uniquely American. In England, the word "tallboy" is used.

High chest A high or tall chest of drawers, starting above the feet.

Hipping A form of cabriole leg used on expensive pieces where the leg continues to a level above the seat-rail.

Hocked legs Cabriole legs are often referred to as "hock" or "hocked" legs.

Holly A hard, white wood with a slightly flecked grain that was used for inlay and stringing. Dyed black it was used as a substitute for ebony.

Honeysuckle Called anthemion. This ornamental honeysuckle motif is derived from a Greek origin. Used by Adam in the eighteenth century.

Hoop-back Type of back design which usually identifies a Queen Anne chair with a curved crest-rail. Also called a yoke-back, but can also refer to a Windsor chair whose back forms a continuous curve or hoop.

Hope, Thomas (1770-1831) Born in Amsterdam and settled in London, he was a designer of Regency furniture. (See Egyptian Revival.)

Hour glass stool A Victorian seat that resembles an hour glass. May have sides of a pleated material.

Huchier Medieval craftsman, with limited ability, who constructed chests and primitive cupboards (hutches).

Hunt table A sideboard table without drawers. Also called a hunt board.

Husk A motif resembling a husk of wheat. Sometimes husks were arranged in swags.

Icicles Geometric inlays shaped like an icicle.

Incised carving Shallow carving. Also called intaglio carving.

Inlay Inserting wood of a contrasting color or texture into the surface of a piece for decoration. When inlay is done in straight lines it is called stringing. Brass is considered an inlay material.

Inset corner   More detailed than a simple notched corner. This corner traces the table top's molded shape. The effect is a contoured pleat.

Intaglio carving   Incised designs. Examples found on Chippendale casepieces.

Intarsia   Inlaid decorative work in which the design is cut out and then placed in corresponding spaces in a veneered or a solid ground.

Invected corner   A pinched or indented corner.

Jacquard   English-Damask tapestries, brocades and all material with elaborate figures requiring the Jacquard loom.

Japanese Revival   From 1870s to 1910.

Japanning   Lacquering of pieces in the Oriental style. In England, this practice began in the seventeenth century.

Jardiniere   French word for a flower stand, or receptacle for flowers such as an urn.

Jig saw   Saw for cutting pierced or fret-work. Originally operated by a treadle. One of first machines to which power was applied.

Kent, William (1684-1748)   Architect and painter. Worked in Palladian style. Designed furniture and mantelpieces.

Keystone   A wedge-shaped detail found on the crest-rails or arches. Examples on Victorian sofas and chairs.

Kidney table   A kidney-shaped table associated with Sheraton.

Kite back   A diamond splat.

Klismos   A classic, Greek type chair with a concave back-rail and curved legs. Important in Neo-Classical designs.

Knee   The outcurved portion of a cabriole leg. It is also called a "hip."

Kneehole   A bureau, with the central portion recessed between two pedestals of drawers. Examples in early eighteenth century.

Knob foot   A small, round, turned foot.

Knobs   Pulls used on drawers and doors of furniture. Round, brass knobs were used from 1795 to 1830. The Victorian period employed many types of pulls such as rosette knobs and glass knobs.

Knotted pine   Wood, originally a second-best plank of timber with rough knots showing. It was used for painted pieces. Today the paint is removed, and these knotted pieces are sold to collectors. Many pieces are fakes produced by persons cashing in on the demand.

Labels   British cabinetmakers have used labels since the eighteenth century.

Lacquered   A finish meant to imitate Oriental lacquer. Important in the seventeenth century.

Ladder-back   This term refers to two different pieces. It can refer to a chair having a number of horizontal slats between its uprights. An early slat-back might be called a ladder-back. It can also refer to a Chippendale chair with shaped, and sometimes pierced or curving horizontal back bars. These chairs are also called "pretzel backs" and "swag backs."

Lambrequin   A short drapery design.

Laminated wood   Thin layers of wood glued together with the grain of each layer at right angles to that above and below.

Lampas   Originally an East Indian printed silk.

Lancet arch   A pointed arch. Examples on Victorian Gothic pieces.

Landscape panel   Description of wood grain that moves in a horizontal direction.

Lappet   A projecting, lapped carving. Examples found on eighteenth century cabriole knees resulting in a raised, carved edge that lapped over the leg.

Lathe-turned   Turning of pieces of wood by rotating them against a tool that shapes them. When the term "turned" is used, as in "turned legs" it means lathe-turned.

Let-in-top   An expensive detail found on various game tables. The top is slightly recessed (dished) to accommodate velvet, needlework or leather, allowing it to lay flush with the surrounding wood area. The top "lets-in" the additional material.

Library table   A large table, often with drawers or space for books, usually on a pedestal. The name for any flat-top desk used for library purposes.

Linen-fold panel   A design for a panel consisting of a combination of straight moldings in the shape of folds of linen. A Gothic design seen on Tudor, Jacobean and Victorian furniture. Examples on chests and screens in Medieval periods.

Linen press   A frame with a wooden spiral screw for pressing linen between two boards.

Lip-molding   Molding that slants downward in a concave curve to a narrow edge. In a cross-section it resembles an upside down thumb. Also called "thumb nail molding."

Lisere French silk, cord fabric made with weft brocaded flowers and warp Jacquard figures.

Livery cupboard A sixteenth and seventeenth century piece with open-work panels or balustered doors for food storage.

Lock plate Metal piece around a lock protecting the keyhole. Also called an escutcheon or scutcheon.

Locker The central, miniature cupboard in the interior of a desk or secretary.

Long chair Also called a daybed.

Looking glass Mirrored glass.

Loop arm A Queen Anne, curved arm.

Loop-back Also called a bow-back. Usually refers to a Windsor chair.

Loose-leaf Table leaf inserted into the opening of an extension table to enlarge its capacity.

Loose seat A slip seat.

Lounge A late nineteenth century sofa or couch. Often these pieces had one arm higher than the other.

Love seat A double chair. A courting chair. "Darby and Joan seat" is the English term; "confidantes" is the French term.

Low-back Name given to a type of Windsor armchair. The back has a horseshoe shaped arm-rail and short spindles.

Low relief Usually applies to shallow carving, or built-up decoration that does not project far from the ground.

Lowboy Usually refers to a low, table-like chest, inspired by the English flat-topped dressing table. The term "lowboy" is American, although it is also used to describe English pieces.

Lozenge A diamond shape. Examples can be seen on early Tudor, Elizabethan and Adam pieces.

Lunette This is a semi-circle, half-moon or fan shape.

Lyre A decorative design found on classical Greek furniture which used the harp as a motif or detail. Thomas Sheraton was particularly fond of this design. The lyre is one of the most recognizable motifs of the Neo-Classical period.

Market value The retail cash value of a piece.

Marlborough foot A square foot found on Chippendale square legs.

Marquetry Contrasting inlay. It can be woods, combined with tortoise shell, brass and mother-of-pearl. The finest marquetry pieces were made in the eighteenth century.

Married piece A piece may be combined of authentic pieces, but has been "made-up" from more than one source. This would not be a fake if it is properly identified. Some married pieces are delightful. Some were "hasty weddings," and others are "living-in-sin." An example would be a chest combined with an open bookcase.

Mask carvings Motif representing a human face, lion or satyr head. Examples on Queen Anne chairs.

Matelasse French meaning to cushion or pad; hence, a quilted surface.

Medallion-back sofa The center of the curved back has a large circular shape enclosed with a wood frame, with cabriole front legs and canted back ones.

Melon foot English bun foot with vertical grooves. The melon foot is not an American foot.

Melon turning A large, round turning which is thick and bulbous. This turning is typical of Elizabethan and Jacobean furniture.

Memory pieces Early pieces of furniture made in America referred to as "memory pieces," because they were made similar to pieces the furniture maker had known before emigrating. Puritan furniture was made in this manner.

Meridienne A short, Victorian daybed or couch with the arms shaped into the upholstered back creating a slope back.

Mitered joint A joint cut at an angle, generally forty-five degrees.

Mixing table Also called a slab table. Originally simple tables, often with inset stone tops, used for mixing. Choice examples have delft tile tops. Later mixing tables often had a storage section on two sides.

Modillion An ornamental cantilever beneath the corona or member of a cornice.

Moire A fabric with a watered silk appearance.

Molded base The base of a casepiece formed of molded elements.

Molded cornice Cornice formed with molded elements.

Moldings Long, narrow, ornamental surfaces that have a profile that casts a shadow.

Monkeyed   A repair or addition, such as a carved shell, for the purpose of making a piece look older or more valuable. An example would be adding inlay to a plain piece.

Monopodium   Classical pedestal support composed of an animal head and a single leg. This design widely used in the early nineteenth century.

Moreen   A coarse, wool material used in the late seventeenth and eighteenth centuries.

Morris, William (1834-1896)   An English painter and furniture designer. In 1861, he founded Morris, Marshall, Franklin & Company. In 1875, this became Morris & Company. Some of the furniture produced by his firm was probably the work of Philip Webb and Ford Madox Brown. The "Morris" chair which became popular in America was probably designed by Ephraim Colman. It had an adjustable bar at the back. Morris style had a great effect on the Arts and Crafts movement. It was inspired by medievalism.

Mortice   A hole or slot made in a piece of furniture that receives a tenon. Found on sixteenth century pieces. A construction element.

Mother-of-pearl   Iridescent inner layer of a shell, usually a nautilus, favored by the Victorians as a decorative inlay for papier-mache. Thin layers of pearl were applied to the surface of a piece, usually in a flower pattern, and japanning was built around this design. Painted decorations and gilding was usually used in conjunction.

Mounts   The brass handles, escutcheons and plates seen on furniture. This word applies to iron work, ormolu, pressed glass and wooden knobs, as well as lock plates and hinges.

Moving sideboard   A design consisting of three tiered trays supported by side brackets and castored. Used to receive dishes and made to move from one area to another. A trolley.

Mule chest Also called a dower chest. A chest with a box above, with one long drawer or two smaller drawers below.

Multiple scooping A round scalloping. Examples are found on early banister back crest-rails.

Muntins Strips of wood that separate and hold glass panes in a furniture door.

Mushroom finials Mushroom shaped turnings. Examples are seen on chair back-posts of slat-back chairs from about 1700.

Mushroom knob A wooden drawer pull that is wider than it is long. It resembles a mushroom.

Nail Piece of metal with a pointed tip and flattened head. Nails have been used in furniture construction for centuries to hold separate pieces together. Nails are also used for decoration. Early board chests were nailed. William and Mary chairs in leather were decorated with nails.

Napoleon bed Also called an "Empire bed" or "sleigh bed." Has curved ends.

Naughty English slang for fake.

Necking Any small band or moulding near the top of a shaft, pillar or column.

Needlepoint Patterns hand worked with a needle using wool or silk, often used as furniture upholstery.

Neo-Classic The use of classical forms during the late eighteenth and early nineteenth century.

Neo-Greek The use of classical Greek forms after the original period. Examples in the Regency period.

Nest of tables Usually four tables that fit together as one or separately.

New Iron Age Name for the Industrial Revolution.

Notched corner An indentation on table top corners.

Nulling Another name for gadrooning. Term used in Jacobean era.

Octagonal top An eight sided top.

Ogee A molding with a single or double cyma curve, having an "S" or double "S" shape. Bracket feet with a cyma curve are ogee. The ogee curve was developed in Greek architecture of the fifth century B.C. Many Chippendale desks and secretaries have ogee bracket feet.

Onion foot A ball shaped foot. Examples on seventeenth century chests.

Onyx tops Usually a table top, a translucent quartz, in a milky or grayish color. Seen on eighteenth century consoles.

Open back A chair back formed by the framing and splat (or splats), and not covered with upholstery.

Open talon A claw-and-ball foot with the claw extending away from the ball.

Ormolu Ormolu is gilded bronze, brass or copper mounts. Ormolu was a French eighteenth century detail. It appeared on English commodes in the 1770s. Greek honeysuckle called anthemion was a frequent motif.

Ottoman Also called a pouf. A tufted, upholstered seat without arms. This piece became important in the Victorian period for seating. It could be rectangular or round. It eventually became an oversized footrest. It was often used in the center of a room. After 1840, they became elaborate. Circular ones might have centers of wood crafting, statuary, lamps or jardinieres.

Outrounded corners The corners of a square or rectangular tabletop where a semi-circular curve replaces a right angle. Examples on Sheraton chests. Called a biscuit-corner on country pieces. Americans called them cookie-corners.

Outset canted corners Corners, usually found on a rectangular top, that are squared and slightly overhung. Found on marble tops of George III side tables.

Ovolo A quarter circle.

Oxbow chest Also called a serpentine or yoke front chest. A chest of drawers having a front which is convex at the sides, and concave in the center without vertical divisions.

Oyster veneer Concentric circles of walnut, yew, elm and mulberry wood used on English pieces. Examples in William and Mary period.

Pad foot A Dutch foot. A rounded, flattish foot resembling a golf club, found on cabriole legs.

Painted furniture Furniture with paint rather than stain applied to the surface. Painted furniture has a history reaching back to the pyramids and was practiced in most countries throughout history.

Paired designs A matched design found on both sides of a piece. Examples are inlaid ovals found on Hepplewhite sideboards.

Palmette   A fan or palm motif. Palm leaf associated with Egyptian design.

Panel   A piece, usually rectangular, that is sunk or raised from the surface. Panel chests were made during the seventeenth century.

Panel chair   A wainscot chair. These were seen in the Tudor period.

Papier-mache   Molded paper pulp that was used for many furniture pieces in the Victorian period. It was suitable for japanning and polishing. Many papier-mache pieces were inlaid with pearl and were also painted with added decorations. Many tilt-top tables were made in this medium. Papier-mache decoration was enhanced around 1825 by the introduction of mother-of-pearl, which was embedded into the varnish before it fully dried. By the 1860s, however, it was outmoded.

Parcel gilding   An ornamental gilding. Partially gilded or stenciled. Examples seen on Queen Anne furniture.

Parisian mounts   French ormolu.

Parlor   The room where families entertained their friends. This was considered a public room.

Parquetry   Inlay in geometric patterns.

Patera   Oval designs found inlaid on Neo-Classical furniture, such as Adam and Hepplewhite pieces.

Patina   This is the mellow quality of color and texture that furniture surfaces, finished or unfinished, acquire with age. Old pieces mellow evenly. If a piece has a glass-like finish, cloudy look or reddish streaks, or all of the above, it is probably French polished. Patinas may not be natural due to chemicals or other unnatural aging effects.

Paw foot Originated in ancient Egypt. Seen on English furniture from the late seventeenth century to the end of the nineteenth century. Examples on Queen Anne chairs (bear or lion).

Peaked arched scroll A scroll, also called a scoop, having a pointed, rounded arch, achieving a tent-like shape. Peaked arch scrolls are found on various scrolled table skirts.

Pear drop A mount, a small pendant introduced in the Restoration period. Ornament (pear shaped) often found on Georgian friezes, such as those of Sheraton in the Georgian period, hanging from the lowest point of an arch.

Pedestal table Table with a central pedestal instead of legs. Examples in the Regency period.

Pediment The ornamental top surmounting a tall casepiece. Some are pointed, some are curved, and some have a broken curve or broken pointed design. On classical Greek or Roman buildings, pediments were triangular.

Peg A wooden pin or dowel that passes through both parts of a mortice and tenon joint to secure it. Very small wooden pegs were sometimes used instead of nails to join parts of desk interiors including the pigeonhole drawers.

Peg-top foot A Sheraton foot resembling a Hepplewhite spade foot, peg-like, and narrowing at the base. Examples on bookcase-top desks.

Pembroke table A drop-leaf table where the central fixed leaf is about twice as wide as the drop-leaves. The drop-leaves are supported on swinging wooden brackets. This type of table was used in the Queen Anne period as a breakfast table. Some still refer to the pembroke table as a breakfast table. The drawer is for eating utensils.

Vocabulary

Pen work Delicate decoration executed with a pen. Some pieces completely covered with pen work.

Pendant finial A downward projecting finial.

Pendant loops A hanging circular or oval device attached to a small head and varying in width from 3/4 inch to 1 inch. Usually found in small drawers between 1740 and 1820.

Pie-crust table A circular, tilt-top table with a raised and carved rim, that stands on a tripod base. The shape of the top resembles a trencher which in turn resembles a Chinese dish. These tables often had pierced edges.

Pier glass A narrow mirror designed to be hung on a wall between windows, often above a pier or console type table.

Pierced bracket A lattice-like bracing decoration.

Pierced splat The back splat of a chair in which details of the design are open.

Pierced talon Also called an open talon.

Pies Circular inlay. Examples found on joints of various Aesthetic Movement cabinets between 1870 and 1880.

Pietro-dure work Panels and table tops composed of semiprecious stones in designs of flowers, birds, shells and arabesques. Examples on Louis XVI style chests, in the Victorian period, that combined ebony wood, ormolu mouldings and pietra-dura panels.

Pigeon hole This is an open storage compartment fitted into the interior of a desk. Usually the interior will have document drawers and a central locker as well as pigeon holes for storage.

Pilaster This is a rectangular or half-round column. Examples on work of William Kent and Thomas Sheraton.

Pile Fabric having a surface made of upright ends as in fur.

Pillar-and-claw table A table with a center pillar or shaft with three or four outcurving legs.

Pin A hardwood dowel.

Pin wheel Decorative motif also called a sunburst, a full sunrise or full fan.

Pinched corner Also called an invected corner.

Pine tree finial A cone-shaped finial.

Pineapple A fruit motif, often used as a finial.

Pinnacle An upright terminal associated with Gothic designs.

Pipe stem turning A turning found on Windsor chair backs resembling a long (smoking) pipe stem.

Plank seat A chair seat made from a single piece of wood.

Platform A late Georgian detail, featuring clustered columns on a platform supported by incurved legs with brass paw feet and casters. This leg design was found on three-part dining tables.

Plinth Block, square or octagonal piece used as a base of a column or chest when solid to the ground.

Plum-pudding Term to describe mahogany with dark elliptical marks.

Plush A fabric like silk, wool or cotton, whose pile is more than 1/8 inch high.

Vocabulary

Pockets   Also called counters, wells and guinea pockets. Seen on game tables.

Poker work   Decorating wood using a heated metal tool in the Victorian period.

Pompeian legs   Victorian period, turned Louis XVI legs that were often decorated with incised carving and applied ornaments, with the largest turning at the top.

Poplin   A silk and worsted material with a corded surface. Early eighteenth century.

Porphyry   A purplish-red stone. Mosaics of porphyry were used on Gothic and Renaissance style nineteenth century pieces.

Porringer top   A table top with cyma shaped corners.

Pot-board   Open shelf, low to the floor on a dresser.

Pouf   A large, Victorian, upholstered stool usually used in the center of a room. A large ottoman.

Press cupboard   The press cupboard is a two part cupboard with a closed top part, and a closed cupboard or drawers in the bottom part.

Pressback   Crest-rails, with pressed designs in imitation of carving, are called pressbacks. Examples on machine-made chairs.

Prie-dieu chair   A chair for kneeling on during prayer, having a high back and a book rest on the top-rail.

Primary wood   The wood which is the material comprising the greatest part or outer surface of a piece.

Prince-of-Wales feathers A motif inspired from the plumes in the Prince of Wales' royal crest. Hepplewhite used this motif in various shield-back chairs. Also seen stamped on Victorian leather chair backs.

Profile The side view or outline of an entire piece or an element such as a moulding.

Prospect door Also called a central locker.

Provenance A written history or pedigree of a piece. It includes who originally owned it, where it was made, when last sold, and so on.

Pugin, Augustus (1812-1852) An English architect and designer. Began with Gothic designs, associated with Arts and Crafts movement.

Pull brackets These are located on either side of the top drawer of a desk or secretary, and are pulled out to support the writing portion. They may be called desk-slides.

Pulvinated skirt Curved skirt with cushion shapes on apron. A Georgian detail.

Punching or punch work Decoration accomplished with a pointed tool. Early brasses were often decorated in this manner. Detail found on Revival pieces.

Putti A motif of a child's head with wings. Examples are found on Victorian beds.

Quadrant brackets Quarter-circle, cast brass brackets which support the fall-front of a desk or secretary.

Quarter-round pilaster This is one quarter of a circular column. It is often reeded, but can be plain.

Quartering A means of obtaining a formal pattern in wood figure by taking four consecutively cut pieces of veneer which have identical figuring, and setting them in opposing form to achieve a mirrored pattern.

Quatrefoil Four intersecting curves, a four leaf clover shape. Examples on Gothic pieces.

Quilloche carving An ornamental band with paired ribbons or lines, flowing in interlaced curves around a series of circular voids. Examples on many English bookcases.

Quirk The narrow groove at the side of a bead.

Rail A horizontal, connecting piece in furniture construction. Chairs have seat-rails, crest-rails, back-rails and stretchers. Rails hold the sides of casepieces together.

Raised edge This is an important design element found on cabriole legs. The design, usually starting near the seat-rail past the edge of the legs, is a raised layer, plain or decorative, such as carved acanthus leaves.

Rake The angle or slant of various furniture legs. Examples are seen on rear furniture legs.

Ram's head Motif found on Adam pieces. Derived from Classical origins.

Rat claw foot Spidery claws surrounding a ball on a cabriole leg.

Ratton Palms of genus calamus. The tough stems used for wickerwork. Often used for bedroom chairs.

Rayed shell A geometric, half-circle design formed with crisp straight (ray) lines.

Recamier sofa A sofa having raised ends. It is French directoire in design, and was named for Madame Recamier. These were also made in the Empire period and called a "Grecian couch." Seen again in the Victorian period.

Recessed stretcher A box stretcher with the front-rail located a little behind the front legs to allow room for the occupant's heels.

Reeding A number of narrow, vertical grooves resembling small convex flutings. Examples are seen on Georgian, Regency and Victorian furniture legs.

Regence style Style of French furnishings, from 1700 to 1720, in which a transition occurs from the Baroque style of Louis XIV to the Rococo style of Louis XV.

Regency Period from 1811 to 1820 during which George, then Prince of Wales, later George IV, was regent of England.

Regilt Means regilded.

Renaissance Period in Europe from the fifteenth to seventeenth century. A rebirth based on art, architecture and philosophy. Designs reborn on English furniture from the sixteenth century.

Rest bed Also a day bed.

Restoration More than repair, restoration means to renew and return a piece to its original state by adding new parts and substituting parts for missing or damaged ones. Restoration is proper and should be respected because without it, many fine pieces would be lost. Good workmanship is extremely important. Valuable pieces can be ruined by inferior craftsmen.

Reverse curve sofa A camel-back, Chippendale piece with a peak on either side of the hump. Examples in Georgian period.

Revivals Designs and styles from previous time periods.

Vocabulary

Ribbon-back A Chippendale chair, with its back composed with twining ribbons. A Rococo design.

Ribs Usually refer to curved elements. Examples on Hepplewhite chairs.

Rim Edge around a table top.

Rinceau An ornamental foliate or floral motif.

Ring and ball A turning of ring and ball elements.

Ring turnings A thick or a thin, circular turning. Ring turnings may be composed of one or many rings.

Rocaille (Rococo) Design of rocks, shells and plant forms. Examples on George II armchairs with carved shells above the arm supports, and on cabriole legs and on the center of the seat-rail.

Rocking chair A unique American design. The rocker was supposedly invented by Benjamin Franklin about 1750. He is said to have placed rockers on an earlier slat-back chair. Rockers are about fourteen to sixteen inches from the ground. In England, rocking chairs were first used in nurseries and for invalids.

Rococo Elaborate ornamentation with luscious curves that combined shell, rocks and rustic naturalistic forms. This rather playful style originated in France about 1720. Thomas Chippendale was influenced by these designs.

Roe Dark flakes in a mahogany figure.

Roll-top desk A desk that closes by use of a flexible cylindrical hood having a convex shape. These are often seen on Victorian desks.

Rolled-arm Arms having an outward curve or roll, seen on chairs and sofas.

Roman arch A semicircular arch or a rounded arch.

Romayne Ornamentation that featured human heads on medallions. Examples on Tudor pieces.

Rope-turned Turning resembling a rope.

Rosette Ornament resembling a rose. A circular detail with curved petals.

Rosette knobs A wood knob, about one inch wide, that projected out about one inch and was decorated with a wood rosette that was about two and one-half inches in diameter.

Round front Also known as elliptic front, swell front or curved front.

Roundabout A corner chair. Also called angle chairs.

Rounded vase turning Wide, vase turning found at top of shaft, often with melon-like reeding. Examples on circa 1850 center tables.

Roundel A round disk, decorative ornament, sometimes incised. Examples are seen on sixteenth century pieces.

Runners Wooden strips attached to the inner sides of a casepiece on which the drawer slides.

Rush seat A furniture seat made of tightly woven or twisted rush.

"S" scroll A double convulute. Examples on seventeenth century cane chairs. A popular Rococo motif.

"S" shaped brackets When large, probably a Queen Anne detail. The large, curved bracket extends over the front-rail and on to the back legs. A dramatic design.

Saber leg Also called a Waterloo leg. Usually on the front legs of a chair, they curve like a saber. Seen on Regency pieces.

Sabot French term for the metal foot to which casters were affixed.

Saddle seat Usually seen on Windsor chairs, a solid wooden seat with a central ridge at the front resembling the pommel on a saddle.

Safari chair A chair that collapsed so a native bearer could carry it. The legs unscrewed from the frame. This piece was often of wicker. Many examples were made in England by Ward & Company from 1880 to 1920.

Salon sets A settee and two armchairs in the Louis XVI style.

Sash plan corner Sheraton's term for ovolo or quarter-circle corners. Examples found on his chests.

Satin One of the basic weave structures in which the filling threads are interlaced with the warp at widely separated intervals, producing the effect of an unbroken surface. Origin Tskinkiang, China.

Satyr masks Mythological male facial design.

Scagliola An imitation stone, from powdered gypsum and glue, that was substituted for marble.

Scaling A carving done to resemble fish scales. A Georgian detail.

Scalloped leaves Serpentine table leaves.

Scalloped top Table top with serpentine edge.

Scoops Also known as guinea pockets and counters. Seen on game tables. May apply to scalloping on aprons or slats.

Scotch chest A typical Edwardian form of chest with drawer edges bevelled or fielded. From 1900 to 1910.

Screws A metal fastener with a tapered shank and slotted head. A handmade screw on an original piece fits tightly and will be hard to remove.

Scroll back A seventeenth century turned chair with scrolled slats.

Scroll ears Scroll shape that may appear on two places. One is on the ends of the crest-rail; the second on the seat-rail at the junction between the leg and the seat-rail. Usually the latter is just called the ear-piece.

Scroll foot A foot which terminates in a tight scrolled form, usually inturning.

Scroll top A curved, broken arch pediment used on casepieces. These are seen on Queen Anne and Chippendale tall casepieces.

Scrolled leg Serpentine curved legs terminating in scrolled feet. Examples on Victorian Rococo tables with marble tops.

Scrubbed Condition of pine table-tops that have been worn smooth and are grayish-white in color from years of washing. These were originally kitchen tables.

Secondary wood Woods that are not visible, such as bracings, backboards and shelves, and are not the same wood as the one used for the outside or for the principal parts of a piece.

Secretary A desk combined with drawers below, and bookcases or shelves in the upper portion. The upper portion may be closed.

Serpentine front A furniture front having a curve that is convex in the middle and ends, but is concave in between.

Serpentine wing An upholstered curved arm. Examples on upholstered chairs.

Serving table A nineteenth century Victorian dining room piece used to supplement the sideboard and usually placed opposite it for already used dishes. In a small room it might replace the sideboard.

Settee A light open seat for two to six persons, having a low back and arms. The Queen Anne, Georgian and Victorian periods had settee pieces.

Settle A wooden bench with an enclosed back and arms. Examples seen in country pieces.

Sewing table A small work table. Examples in the seventeenth and eighteenth century.

Shaft A stem, pillar or column support found on tables.

Shell design A seashell design. Called a sunburst and a fan. Important on Queen Anne furniture.

Sheraton, Thomas (1751-1806) An English cabinetmaker in the Georgian period. The American Sheraton period is named for him.

Shoe A disk or cushion underneath the foot of a piece of furniture. These can be seen on Queen Anne pad feet. The term also refers to the piece between the seat-rail and the splat. A chair with the splat and shoe as one piece will not usually be an antique.

Shoulder-pieces The pieces glued at two sides of the top of a cabriole leg. They avoid an abrupt termination at the top of the leg. Also referred to as an ear-piece.

Show-wood The wood that shows on upholstered pieces.

Shuttle lunette A design found on seventeenth century chests composed of opposing lunettes.

Side chair Side chairs, having no arms, stood with their backs to the wall when not in use. So named because they stood originally beside a wall.

Side table A table designed to stand against (beside) a wall.

Sideboard Usually a dining room piece with shelves and drawers. Examples in Adam, Hepplewhite and Sheraton designs.

Silk Cloth made from the lustrous fiber obtained as a filament from the cocoon of the silk worm. Origin: China.

Skinned A piece that has had its paint removed.

Skirt Also called an apron.

Slab table An eighteenth century table with a stone or marble top. Sometimes called a mixing table.

Slat-back chair A turned chair with a back of horizontal, concave slats. Made from the seventeenth century to the present.

Sleigh bed Also called a Napoleon bed or an Empire bed. Has curved ends.

Slide A large, pull out shelf on chests for brushing clothes. Also a small slide to hold a candle.

Vocabulary

Sliding well Portion of a slant-top desk interior (usually the center section) that moves or slides out. Designed to conceal a secret or used as a place for hiding coins or valuables.

Slip covers Appeared in the seventeenth century when upholstered furniture commenced.

Slip seat An upholstered seat that can be removed.

Slipper chair A chair characterized by a low seat. Usually an upholstered bedroom chair used for putting on slippers. A slipper chair does not have Dutch slipper feet unless designed with them.

Slipper foot A Dutch or club type pad foot with a pointed toe. English slipper feet are less pointed than American ones. The snake foot is often called a slipper foot on English pieces.

Slips The boards that fitted into a circular nineteenth century dining table when extended to enlarge it. Drawer slips which are between the drawer side and drawer bottom.

Snake foot A form of Dutch foot having an elongated pad foot, but with the toe resembling a snake's head. These have a cushion. Examples are seen on Georgian tripod tables. The English often call them slipper feet. Americans would only call them snake feet.

Sociable A Victorian piece with separate seating sections. Could be two, three or four parts. Examples in the Louis XVI style.

Socked foot Also called a stockinged pad foot. A Queen Anne detail. Vertical, sometimes lobed, carving emanating from the simple pad or ribbed foot to above the ankle. A horizontally carved top to the stocking appears on some cabriole legs while others have only vertical or lobed carving. May be seen on revival pieces.

Sofa Developed from the daybed and double chairs.

Spade foot A rectangular tapered foot. Carved spade feet are English, not American. Examples on Hepplewhite pieces.

Spandrel The space enclosed by two surfaces at right angles, or between an arch and its frame, frequently filled with small fretted ornament or inlaid fans.

Spanish foot Also called the Braganza foot. Named for Catherine of Braganza who became the queen of Charles II. Also called a knurl or a Portuguese Flemish scroll foot. A curved-under foot that is found on turned, blocked and cabriole legs. If the foot does not turn under, it may be called a brush foot, but often the turned portion has been damaged. Spanish feet often display a carved or applied bracelet at the ankle. (Also called a collar, cuff or wrister.) These feet are seen on seventeenth century pieces. It is said that the inspiration came from bound feet seen on Oriental women. Cabriole legs with Spanish feet may also display a garter.

Spider legs Very thin, turned legs. Examples on Georgian tables.

Spindles Slender turned pieces of wood. Examples may be seen forming the backs of Windsor chairs. Spindles are also seen on aesthetic Victorian pieces.

Spiral leg A leg resembling a twisted rope. Also called a barley or sugar twist of Portuguese or Indian origin.

Spiral turning A twisted turning often seen on English furniture. Also called sugar twist and barley twist turning. Seen on Elizabethan style pieces.

Spitalfields silk A woven silk. Product of Spitalfields, London, from the early seventeenth century.

Vocabulary

Splat The central vertical panel of a chair back. Examples on Queen Anne chairs.

Splay leg A leg that flares out.

Split spindle An ornament of the seventeenth century applied to cabinets and cupboards.

Spool Turning in the shape of a row of spools. It was used mostly for legs. It was introduced after 1820, and continued to be used through the Victorian period. Spool beds were very popular.

Spool-turned beds Made of turned spools, popular on mid-Victorian Elizabethan style furniture such as beds and chairs.

Spoon-back A vase splat shaped more like a spoon than a vase. A chair back with a round top and a narrow waist.

Squab A loose cushion. These were used on medieval seats.

Stem Another name for a shelf, pillar or column support on a table.

Step-back Country term for a cupboard with its upper part set a "step" back from its lower section.

Step-top A step or steps above the cornice on flat-top Queen Anne highboys.

Stepped curve A stop in the direction of a curve. Seen in the uprights of Queen Anne and early Georgian pieces.

Stick back Another name for Windsor chairs.

Stile The vertical member in panel furniture. The stile is the outer upright on a piece of furniture.

Stop-fluting Concave fluting alternating with convex fluting.

Stopped-in-mid-air An 1890 term that describes elements, such as a chair back, that do not appear complete.

Straight front A flat-front casepiece.

Strapwork Intertwined designs seen on Renaissance pieces. Examples appear in the Tudor period on chests.

Stretcher The crosspiece which connects and braces furniture legs.

Stretcher table A large, rectangular, Tudor table with turned legs joined by rectangular stretchers. It was called a "long joined table."

Stringing Thin bands of inlay for decoration.

Strong waist molding When the molded element on the lower chest of a chest-on-chest is bold.

Stuff-over chair One in which the upholstery covers the seat-rails.

Stump foot Foot which is not a separate portion from the leg, but a slight outward curve which continues directly to the floor.

Subbing Substituting new pieces on an antique for repairs or for deception.

Sunburst The favorite English word to describe a sunrise, rising sun, fan or shell motif.

Sunrise crest-rail A convex top-rail in a fan shape and design.

Supporting column A column at the front corner of a casepiece which supports an overhanging frieze drawer.

Suspended inlay   Hanging inlay usually attached to a top element such as the top of a leg.

Swan's-neck   A curved, broken scroll. Examples topping tall casepieces.

Swan's-neck handle   The brass pull (handle) on a brass plate, with a convex center curve is called a swan's-neck, bail, pull or handle. Examples on early Georgian pieces.

Swell-front   Convex-curved front.

Swelled bracket foot   An outward curved bracket foot. Examples on various Chippendale casepieces, and almost always on bombé pieces.

Swing-leg   A hinged leg that supports a drop-leaf.

Tabby   A rich, silk fabric with a wavy figure that was manufactured after the Restoration period.

Tablet chair   Also called a writing armchair. An armchair with one flat arm that is used as a writing surface. In the eighteenth century, various Windsors have this detail.

Tallboy   The English term to describe a high chest or a chest-on-a-frame. Called highboys in America.

Tambour   A flexible sliding shutter constructed of thin strips of wood that are glued to a coarse woven backing. Tambour desks were the ancestors of the modern roll-top desks. Sheraton called bureaus with this detail "cylinder desks."

Tang   A wire strip of wrought iron bent to attach teardrop and bail handles. Examples in Stuart period.

Tassel feet   Found on rare Chinese Chippendale tables, with Rococo and Gothic motifs. These feet resemble tassels.

Tavern table   A table with no leaves. It is usually rectangular and has square or turned legs. These tables were usually braced with a solid stretcher. Originally tavern tables were intended for use in a public place.

Tea table   Appears in the late Stuart period. They continued to be important in the Queen Anne period, and on into the Georgian period. Some were rectangular with tray tops and four legs. Queen Anne pieces had cabriole legs. Some were tilt-and-turn tables standing on tripod legs. Tea drinking, an important social function, took place in the main room where the tables were placed. This was not a dining room piece.

Teapoy   Small table on a single support usually with a box or tea caddy forming the top.

Teardrop brasses   Furniture mounts that were made of cast brass and had pendant handles shaped like a teardrop. These brasses first appeared in the late Stuart period. Some were decorated with punched or chased designs.

Tenon   This is a thin projecting piece that fits into a corresponding groove to unite two elements. Construction element found on medieval pieces.

Term   A statue or bust of the upper body, minus arms, terminating in a pedestal. Examples in Adam period.

Term figures   Term figures are like pedestal terns, which are statues or busts of the upper body, no arms. They may have feet terminating in a pedestal and are found flanking various Regency cabinets.

Tête a tête   Two attached Victorian chairs positioned for courting, often facing in opposite directions. Some small sofas were also called tête a têtes.

Vocabulary

Thonet, Michael (1796-1871)   Born in Germany; worked in Vienna. Designed classic bentwood furniture that was popular in England.

Thrown chair   Another name for a lathe-turned chair.

Thumb nail   Molding that slants downward in a concave curve to a narrow edge. In a cross section, resembles an upside down thumb. Also referred to as thumb molding.

Tier tables   Small tables with more than two tops arranged one above the other.

Till   A covered compartment that was used to store small possessions found in various early chests close to the top. They were made of oak or pine on early chests.

Tilt-top table   A tripod table with a circular, square, clover-leaf or octagon top, hinged to tilt vertically. They are seldom shorter than twenty-eight inches.

Tip-and-turn table   Tripod tables whose top can rotate as well as tip vertically.

Toe rest   An upholstered pad, for toes, at center of crossed-stretchered desks, usually for ladies in the Victorian period.

Tongue and groove joint   Used for joining two timbers. On one side is a continuous bead-like molding, and on the other is a channel into which the bead-like molding fits.

Top-rail   Top horizontal rail of a chair or sofa.

Torus molding   A bold, convex molding.

Tracery   Designs of arcs and circles in intricate patterns. Examples on Chippendale Gothic pieces.

Transitional furniture Furniture with details from two contiguous periods. This is why it is important to know the major periods and the order in which they appear. The latest characteristics on a piece determine its period.

Tray-top A table top with a raised molded edge resembling a tray.

Trefoil A three-arched, or fleur de lis shape. Examples on Gothic designs.

Trellis work A lattice design or fret-work. Examples on Chippendale furniture.

Trestle supports Rigid frames that support planks resulting in a trestle table. Examples in Tudor period. Also as Regency supports, often with scrolling inlay, on paw or bun feet.

Trestle table A table composed of a fixed leaf supported by two or three trestles instead of legs. Tudor trestle tables were simply a wide board placed over trestles, and when not in use taken apart.

Triangular base A base in triangular form. Examples on Regency tripod tables with a carved stem attached to a triangular base.

Triangular chair A three-legged chair.

Trifid foot A Dutch foot also called a "ribbed foot."

Triglyph An architectural separating device found on Doric friezes. On Victorian furniture these grooves or half-grooves may appear on Rococo pieces on each side of an astragal shaped crest-rail.

Tripod table A table with a pedestal supported by three canted or outcurved legs. Tripod tables developed from candle stands. Tripod construction is very sure-footed.

Vocabulary

Trolley A moving sideboard.

Trumpet leg A turned leg that resembles an upturned trumpet. These legs were seen on William and Mary casepieces and tables. Trumpet turnings were also combined with vase and inverted cup turnings. Trumpet-turned legs are rarer than cup turnings.

Tub chair Late eighteenth century easy chair, with a round back and wide wings.

Tufting The tying down of an upholstered surface by means of a button sewed through the upholstery. The arrangement and resulting folds produces a pattern.

Tulip ornament A seventeenth century ornament and design element important when tulips were expensive in Holland. Examples carved on early chests.

Turkish cozy corner Looping of Oriental textiles, pierced metal lamps, mountains of pillows and furniture inlaid with pearl that provided a "Turkish" ambiance during the Victorian period.

Turning Shaping of wood on a lathe with the help of turning chisels.

Turnip foot A variation of the ball foot; resembles a turnip. Some have a collar at the base.

Turret corners Outrounded or outcurved corners. They may descend to the furniture leg or merely extend past the table top. Examples on eighteenth century game tables.

Turtle-back Half-oval turned decoration seen on Jacobean pieces. Also called an egg, boss or jewel.

Twist-reeded columns An early Victorian detail often with faceted sections similar to the pineapple design. Examples seen on chests.

Twist turning Double rope or barley twist. Important in the seventeenth century.

Tympanum arch The recessed space between the horizontal and the sloping cornice of a pediment.

U form Found on Victorian slipper chairs. The back has a padded U form with the curved section facing the seat.

Underframe The furniture part which is supported by the legs.

Undulating seat-rail A wavy seat-rail found on Rococo style sofas with scrolled feet.

Unnatural patina A wood surface showing the result of refinishing, French polishing or other unnatural devices.

Uprights A vertical member such as a chair stile. Also may refer to a Victorian chair with a high upholstered back.

Urn A decorative vase usually with a pedestal used as a finial or as a finial with a blaze.

Valance A skirt; also represents drapery. When it represents a drapery, it is often called a lambrequin design or a swag.

Vase-and-ring turned Turning that combines vase and ring shapes.

Vase-shaped splat A chair splat with a vase shape. A very slender vase shape is called a spoon shape.

Veneer A thin layer of wood glued to a base wood. Veneer is also called "thin skin." Used throughout the eighteenth century. Early examples from ancient Egypt.

Venture furniture Furniture made for speculation and sold in places far from origin.

Vernacular furniture Term used to describe furniture imitating high style pieces with features already out of date.

Victorian period English 1830-1900; American 1840-1910; French 1848-1914.

Victorian upright Refers to a high-back, upholstered Victorian chair.

Vitrine A display cabinet, glazed on the front and often on all sides. Many examples on Louis XVI Revival styles.

Vitruvian scroll A repeat of "C" scrolls creating a wave shape. Examples on eighteenth century furniture.

Volute A spiral, ornamental scroll.

Volute ears Scroll carved ears.

Volute foot Outward scrolling foot that is associated with Baroque furniture.

Wainscot furniture Furniture built with a frame inset with panels. This is architectural furniture. Tudor and Stuart furniture used wainscot construction.

Wall furniture All furniture designed to stand against a wall. Examples are secretaries, highboys and bookcases.

Wardrobes A piece of furniture for holding clothes. Developed from the cupboard and cabinet in the late seventeenth century.

Water leaf An ornamental design derived from a laurel leaf.

Web foot A Dutch ribbed, or trifid foot.

Wellington chest Made as a specimen chest from 1830 to 1885. A tall, narrow piece with perhaps ten drawers. There is no reason to have named them for the Duke. Many were designed in oak with medieval style machine carving.

Whatnot A display cabinet. American term for a piece with open shelves for bric-a-brac, often carved, and important in the Victorian period. The French word is "etagere." Also made as a corner piece.

Wheat ears An ornamental detail showing several ears of wheat often carved in low relief, high relief and inlaid.

Wheel back An oval back with a central patera or disk, with spokes radiating from the center. Examples on George III chairs.

White wood Natural or unfinished wood.

Whorl foot A foot carved in the shape of an upcurved scroll when the leg ends in an outward, upturned scroll. Seen on various Chippendale pieces. These also appear on Victorian pieces with a French Rococo flavor.

William Morris & Company An English company that designed and made good quality commercial furniture and furnishings (like wallpaper) during the Victorian period. Their finest pieces are Arts and Crafts designs inspired by medievalism.

Willow brasses Brass mounts with plates that are baroque scrolled in outline. They were also made in open pierced patterns. Examples on late Queen Anne and Chippendale pieces.

Windsor chair Associated with the High Wycombe Bucks region. Made of turned members with a saddle seat. First seen in the Queen Anne period.

Vocabulary

Windsor rocker A comb back chair with rockers, said to have been invented by Benjamin Franklin. A uniquely American design. Although the Windsor was first made during the reign of Queen Anne, Franklin turned it into a rocking chair.

Wing chair Also called a fireside chair or an easy chair. Popular from the seventeenth century. Usually upholstered.

Winged finials Urn finials with wings instead of handles, resembling a trophy cup. Examples found on Victorian Renaissance style beds on the upright supports.

Winged monopodia supports Winged animals, dolphins, griffins or giant wings featuring one leg.

Winged paw An animal foot with winged carving appearing on its knee.

Wire furniture Furniture made of wire. Competed in the Victorian period with cast-iron furniture. Used as garden furniture, plant stands and serving pieces.

Wishbone mirror A "Y" or wishbone shaped frame enclosing a mirror. Some were attached to a chest.

Wool terry Wool with rows of loops on face, back or both sides. Used in color on parlor suites of 1876.

Work table A table made in the last half of the eighteenth century for women's sewing tools. Work tables were made in many revival styles in the Victorian period. Some were made of papier-mache.

Writing arm A wide, wooden piece, curved on one side, attached to the right arm of a chair for writing. Examples seen on various Windsor chairs.

"X" form splat   A splat, existing of an "X," found on George III armchairs.

"X" form stretcher   Also called a satire.

Yoke back   A crossbar with two S-shaped curves used as the top-rail of chair backs in Queen Anne and Georgian periods. Has an ox-yoke shape, a bow or concave shape. Another name for a Queen Anne hoop-back chair.

Yoke-rail   A top-rail on a yoke back.

BIBLIOGRAPHY

Ackerman, Martin S. *Smart Money and Art*. Barrytown, NY: Station Hill Press, 1986.

Andrews, Edward D., and Faith Andrews. *Shaker Furniture*. New York: Dover Publications, 1964.

Andrews, John. *The Price Guide to Antique Furniture*. England: Baron Publishing and the Antique Collectors' Club, 1980.

Aronson, Joseph. *The Book of Furniture and Decoration*. New York: Crown Publishers, 1936.

———. *The Encyclopedia of Furniture*. New York: Crown Publishers, 1938.

Athearn, Robert. *American Heritage*. Vol. 1. New York: Dell Publishing Co., 1963.

Bates, Elizabeth, and Jonathan Fairbanks. *American Furniture*. New York: Marek Publishing Co., 1981.

Beck, Doreen. *American Furniture*. London: Hamlyn Publishing Group Ltd., 1975.

Bishop, Robert. *How to Know American Antique Furniture*. New York: E.P. Dutton, 1973.

Bles, Arthur de. *Genuine Antique Furniture*. New York: Garden City Publishing, 1929.

Blundell, Peter, and Phil Dunning. *Marketplace Guide to Victorian Furniture*. Paducah, KY: Collector Books, 1981.

Bramwell, Martyn, ed. *International Book of Wood*. New York: Simon and Schuster, 1976.

Cescinsky, Herbert. *The Gentle Art of Faking Furniture*. New York: Dover Publication, Inc., 1967.

Cescinsky, Herbert and George Leland Hunter. *English and American Furniture*. New York: Garden City Publishing Co., 1929.

Chippendale, Thomas. *The Gentleman and Cabinet-Maker's Director*. 1794. Reprint. New York: Dover Publications, 1969.

Columbia Encyclopedia, 2nd edition.

Comstock, Helen. *American Furniture*. New York: Viking Press, 1962.

Comstock, Helen, and L.A. Ramsey. *Antique Furniture*. New York: Hawthorn Books, 1969.

Connell, Neville. "The Early Furniture of Barbados." *Magazine Antiques* (May 1961): 458-62.

Corbin, Patricia. *All About Wicker*. New York: E.P. Dutton, 1978.

Coscinsky, Herbert. *English Furniture of the Eighteenth Century*. London: The Waverly Book Co., 1911.

Coward, John Mebane. *Art Nouveau*. New York: McCann, Inc., 1950.

Decorative Art of Victoria's Era. New York: Charles Scribner's Sons, 1950.

Dreppered, Carl. *Victorian, the Cinderella of Antiques*. New York: Doubleday Co., 1950.

Fales, Dean, Jr. *American Painted Furniture 1660-1880*. New York: E.P. Dutton and Co., 1972.

Fastnedge, Ralph. *English Furniture Styles from 1500-1830*. New York: A.S. Barnes Co., 1962.

Fenmore, Donald. "American Metals." Lecture presented at the Art Institute, Chicago, February 7, 1988.

Fitzgerald, Oscar. *Three Centuries of American Furniture*. Englewood Cliffs, NJ: Prentice Hall, Inc., 1982.

Furniture for the Victorian Home. England: A. J. Downing, 1833.

Furniture. Vol. 2. Washington: William C. Cooper, Hewitt, Ketchum, and Smithsonian Museums, 1981.

Gaines, Edith. "Collector's Notes." *Magazine Antiques* (January 1964): 110-11.

Gilbert, Christopher. "Chippendales's Patrons in Yorkshire." *Magazine Antiques* (January 1990): 308-23.

Girauard, Mark. "The Power House." In *The Treasure House of Britain*. London: Yale University Press, 1985.

Grow, Lawrence, and Dian Von Zwech. *American Victorian*. New York: Harper and Row, 1984.

Grotz, George. *Grotz's Antique Furniture Styles*. New York: Doubleday and Co., 1987.

_____. *The Furniture Doctor*. New York: Doubleday and Co., 1983.

Hagerty, Francis. *Make Your Own Antiques*. Boston: Little Brown and Co., 1975.

Hamilton, Charles. *Auction Madness*. New York: Everest House Publications, 1981.

Hayward, Charles. *Antique or Fake*. New York: St. Martins Press, 1970.

Hayward, John. "Chinese Export & English Chinoiserie Furniture." *Magazine Antiques* (February 1961): 177-80.

Hayward, Helena. *World Furniture*. New York: McGraw Hill, 1965.

Heckscher, Morrison H. *American Furniture in the Metropolitan Museum of Art*. Vol. 1. New York: Metropolitan Museum of Art and Random House, 1985.

Hinckley, F. *Directory of Historic Cabinet Woods*. New York: Crown Publishing, 1960.

Hornung, Clarence. *Treasury of American Design*. New York: Abrams, Inc., 1972.

Hughes, Therle. *Old English Furniture*. New York: MacMillon Co., 1963.

Jervis, Simon. *Victorian Furniture*. London: Ward Lock and Co., Ltd., 1968.

Kirk, John. *American Furniture and the British Tradition to 1830*. New York: Alfred Knopf, 1982.

Kovel, Ralph, and Terry Kovel. *American Country Furniture 1780-1875*. New York: Crown Publishing Co., 1965.

———. *Kovel's Know Your Antiques*. New York: Crown Publishers, 1981.

Lavine, Sigmund. *Handmade in England*. New York: Dodd Mead & Co., 1968.

Lichten, Frances. *Decorative Art of Victoria's Era*. New York: Charles Scribner's and Sons, 1950.

MacDonald, Margaret. *English Furniture*. New York: G.P. Putman's Sons, 1965.

McClinton, Katharine. *An Outline of Period Furniture*. New York: Clarkson Palter, Inc., 1972.

Michie, Thomas S., and Christopher P. Monkhouse. "Pattern Books in the Redwood Library and Athanaeum, Newport, Rhode Island." *Magazine Antiques* (January 1990): 286-99.

Miller, E. *American Antique Furniture*. Vol. 1 and 2. New York: Barrows and Co., 1988.

Miller, Judith, and Martin Miller, eds. *The Antiques Directory Furniture*. New York: Portland House, 1985.

Nutting, Wallace. *Furniture Treasury*. Vol. 1. New York: MacMillian Co., 1948.

Oates, Phyliss Bennet. *The Story of Western Furniture*. Vol 1. New York: Harper Row, 1981.

Ormsbee, Thomas. *Field Guide to Early American Furniture*. Boston: Little Brown Co., 1952.

Ormsbee, T.H., and R.W. Symonds. *Antique Furniture of the Walnut Period*. New York: Robert M. McBride and Co., 1947.

Pinto, Edward H. "English Rent & Library Tables." *Magazine Antiques* (June 1962): 626-29.

Ramsey, L.G., ed. *The Complete Encyclopedia of Antiques Compiled by the Connoisseur*. New York: Hawthorn Books, Inc., 1962.

Random House College Dictionary of the English Language, 1966 edition.

Riley, Noel, ed. *World Furniture*. London: Octopus Books Limited, 1980.

Rogers, John. *English Furniture*. Middlesex, England: Spring Books, 1967.

Sack, Albert. *Fine Paints of Furniture*. New York: Crown Publishers, Inc., 1950.

Sack, Harold. "Authenticating American Eighteenth-Century Furniture." *Magazine Antiques* (May 1985): 749-22.

Salomonsky, Verna Cook. *Masterpieces of Furniture*. 3rd ed. New York: Dover Publications, 1974.

Savage, George. *Antiques, Fakes and Reproductions*. London: Barrie & Rockliff, 1963.

Schiffer, Herbert, and Nancy Schiffer. *Woods We Live with*. Exton, PA: Schiffer Ltd., 1977.

Shaker. Washington: Smithsonian Institution Press, 1973.

Shull, Thelma. *Victorian Antiques*. Rutland, VT: Charles E. Tuttle Co., 1963.

Siegel, Jeanne. *How to Speak Furniture with an Antique American Accent*. Chicago: Bonus Books, 1991.

———. *How to Speak Furniture with an Antique Victorian Accent*. Chicago: Bonus Books, 1991.

Sotheby's Guide. Vol. 5. England: Penguin Books, 1990.

Swedberg, Harriett, and Robert Swedberg. *Victorian Furniture*. Des Moines, IA: Wallace Homestead, 1976.

Symond, R.W. *English Furniture*. England: Antique Collector's Club, 1980.

Symond, R.W., and B.B. Whineray. *Victorian Furniture*. London: Studio Editions, 1987.

Taylor, Margaret McDonald. *British Furniture*. New York: G.P. Putnam & Sons, 1966.

Thornton, Peter. *Seventeenth Century Interior Decoration in England*. New Haven, CT: Yale Universtiy Press, 1981.

Thomas, Gertrude. "Cane, a Tropical Transplant." *Magazine Antiques* (January 1961): 92-5.

Toynbe, Arnold. *Half the World*. New York: Holt, Rinehart and Winstor, 1973.

Watkinson, Ray. *William Morris as Designer*. New York: Reinhold Publishing Co., 1967.

Wills, Geoffrey. *English Furniture 1760-1900*. New York: Doubleday & Co., 1971.

Yates, Raymond. *Antique Fakes*. New York: Grammercy's Publishing Co., 1950.

Yates, Raymond F., and Marquerite Yates. *A Guide to Victorian Antiques*. New York: Harper and Row, 1949.

INDEX

A

acacia wood, 38
Adam, Robert, 10, 58-60, 87
amboyna wood, 38
ambry, 47
American Tories, 33
Anglo-Japanese, 6, 18-9, 24, 88
Anne, Queen, 14, 53-4
applewood, 38
applied decoration, 89
appraisal, 45
architectural furniture, 90
arks, 46
arkwright, 13, 46
Art Nouveau, 90
Arts and Crafts, 70, 90
ash wood, 38
auction prices, 74-83
auctions, 41-3, 71-3

B

backboards, 19
back stool, 50-1
Barbados, 15
barber's chair, 15-6
beau brummell, 16
beechwood, 60, 69
beeswax, 49
bentwood, 69, 133
birch, 38
blacksmithing, 50
bog oak, 38
boxwood, 38
Braganza feet, 18-9, 52

brasses, 27-8, 31-2
brass inlay, 139
Bullock, George, 64-5

C

calamander, 38
cane chairs, 18
card tables, 102
Carolean, 5, 102
carpenter's guild, 12
carving, 20, 27, 47-8, 56, 64, 67
cedar, 38
center table, 103
Charles I, 5
Charles II, 5, 17, 49
cherry, 38
chest, 12, 13, 46
Chinese, 14, 55-8, 65
chinoiserie, 14, 105
Chippendale, 10, 16, 19-20, 55-62, 105
Cobb, John, 58
coffers, 46
Commonwealth, 5
court cupboard, 48
court furniture, 14
Coxed, John, 54
Craft Movement, 109
Cromwell, Oliver, 5
Cromwell, Richard, 5
Cromwellian chair, 15
cypress wood, 38

D

davenport, 112
deal, 19
directoire, 113-4
dovetails, 28, 115
drawers, 19-20, 31, 115-6
drink board, 17
dust-boards, 22, 117

E

Eastlake, Charles, 118
ebony, 39
Edward VI, 4
Edward VII, 17
Edwardian, 119
Egyptian Revival, 64-5
Elizabeth I, 4, 49
Elizabethan design, 67-8
elm wood, 39, 48
English country house, 2
Exhibition of 1851, 67
experimental furniture, 67

F

fakes, 26-7, 44
fantasy furniture, 69, 121
farthingale chair, 50-1, 121
fir wood, 39
French polishing, 33, 123
French Rococo, 67-8

G

Gainsborough chair, 22, 124
Garrick, David, 16
George I, 6, 17, 54
George II, 6, 17
George III, 6, 7, 17
George IV, 7, 17, 64
Georgian, 6, 7, 54-63
Gillow, 59
Goodison, Benjamin, 54, 58

Gothic designs, 55-7, 67
great hall, 12
Gumley, John, 54

H

Hallet, William, 58
Harewood House, 59
harlequin furniture, 62
Henry VII, 4, 10
Henry VIII, 4
Hepplewhite, George, 10, 21, 59-63, 127
herringbone, 9
Hope, Thomas, 64
house sales, 72-3
huchier, 47, 128
Huguenots, 50

I

Ince, William, 58
Industrial Revolution, 66-7
iron, 46

J

Jacobean, 4, 18
jacquard, 129
James I, 4, 49
James II, 5
japanning, 20, 51-2
Jennens & Betridge, 69
joining, 46-7, 50, 57

K

Kent, William, 129
kingwood, 39

L

labels, 30
lacquer, 51-2
lignum vitae, 39

limewood, 39
Linnell, William, 58
livery cupboard, 132
Louis XV, 68
Louis XVI, 67
lyre, 133

M

Mackintosh, Charles, 69
mahogany, 35-7, 57, 64
marble industry, 67
market value, 45
marquetry, 20, 50
Mary I, 4
Mary II, 5
Mayhew, John, 58
Moore, James, 54
Morris, William, 69, 135
mother-of-pearl, 24, 135
mounts, 31-2
mulberry wood, 35

N

nails, 29, 136
Neo-Greek, 68
Nostell Priory, 59

O

oak wood, 35, 37, 50
ogee, 137
olive wood, 39
Oriental influences, 68

P

paint, 29, 48-9, 138
Palladian, 22
papier-mache, 24, 67, 68-9, 139
pear wood, 39
pine conifer, 39
plywood, 39

press cupboard, 48
provenance, 45
Pugin, Augustus, 144
Puritan, 18
purplewood, 39

R

recamier sofa, 145
Regence style, 146
Regency, 7, 64-5, 62, 146
Renaissance designs, 10, 68
rent tables, 16
restoration, 44
Richard II, 9-10
rocking chairs, 23
rosewood, 37, 62
Ruskin, William, 70

S

satinwood, 35, 37
screws, 28-9
Seddon, 59
Shakers, 15
Sheraton, Thomas, 10, 17, 22-3, 59, 61-4, 151
Spanish foot, 52, 154
Stuart, 4, 5, 46-52
Stuart, James, 59
sycamore, 40

T

textiles, 13
The Tatler, 15
Thonet, Michael, 69
thuja wood, 40
transitional, 44-5
tripod stool, 12
Tudor, 4, 46-9
tulip wood, 40, 60

V

veneer, 29, 34-5, 51, 64
Victoria, 8
Victorian, 8, 23, 65, 66-70
Vile, William, 58
Vosey, C.F.A., 69

W

walnut, 34-5, 37
Washington, Martha, 22
Wellington chest, 164
Welsh dresser, 14
white maple, 40
wicker, 51
William III, 5
William IV, 7, 17
William and Mary, 14, 52
William Morris & Co., 164
Windsor, 20, 164
woods, 33, 37-40
wood sculptors, 13
Woster, T., 54

X

"x"-frame chairs, 51
"x" stretchers, 52

Y

yew wood, 40, 50

Z

zebra wood, 40

Too Good to Miss
from Bonus Books

How to Speak Furniture with an Antique Victorican Accent
By Jeanne Siegel
Paper, 171 pages $12.95

How to Speak Furniture with an Antique American Accent
By Jeanne Siegel
Paper, 213 pages $12.95

Everybody's Guide To Plate Collecting
Increase enjoyment and profits
By Herschell Lewis & Margo Lewis
Paper, 212 pages $9.95

Please send me:

_____copies *How to Speak Furniture with an Antique Victorian Accent* at $12.95

_____copies *How to Speak Furniture with an Antique American Accent* at $12.95

_____copies *Everybody's Guide to Plate Collecting* at $9.95

☐ **Check Enclosed** (please add $3.00 shipping & handling)
☐ **VISA**
☐ **MasterCard**
☐ **American Express**

Card Number _____
Expiration Date _____
Signature _____

Mail your orders to: **Bonus Books**
160 E. Illinois St.
Chicago, IL 60611
or CALL
1-800-225-3775
Illinois residents please add 8% sales tax